ITIL®

Best Management Practice

Key Element Guide
ITIL® Service Design

D0802625

London: TSO

information & publishing solutions

Published by TSO (The Stationery Office)
and available from:

Online
www.tsoshop.co.uk

Mail, Telephone, Fax & E-mail
TSO
PO Box 29, Norwich, NR3 1GN
Telephone orders/General enquiries:
0870 600 5522
Fax orders: 0870 600 5533
E-mail: customer.services@tso.co.uk
Textphone 0870 240 3701

TSO@Blackwell and other Accredited Agents

First edition Crown Copyright 2008

Second edition Crown Copyright 2012

First published 2012

ISBN 9780113313617 (Single copy ISBN)
ISBN 9780113313662 (Sold in a pack of 10
copies)

Printed in the United Kingdom for The
Stationery Office

Material is FSC certified. Sourced from fully
sustainable forests.

P002500761   c18   22330   07/12

Contents

Acknowledgements

AUTHOR

Lou Hunnebeck, Third Sky Inc.

KEY ELEMENT GUIDE AUTHORING TEAM

David Cannon, BMC Software

Ashley Hanna, HP

Vernon Lloyd, Fox IT

Stuart Rance, HP

Randy Steinberg, Migration Technologies Inc.

REVIEWERS

Best Management Practice and The Stationery Office would like to thank itSMF International for managing the quality assurance of this publication, and the following reviewers for their contributions:

Duncan Anderson, Global Knowledge; John Donoghue, Allied Irish Bank plc; John Earle, itSMF Ireland Ltd; Robert Falkowitz, Concentric Circle Consulting; Padraig Farrell, SureSkills; Siobhan Flaherty, Generali PanEurope; Signe Marie Hernes Bjerke, Det Norske Veritas; Michael Imhoff Nielsen, IBM; Jackie Manning, Bord Gáis Networks; Krikor Maroukian, King's College London; Reiko Morita, Ability InterBusiness Solutions, Inc.; Trevor Murray, The Grey Matters; Gary O'Dwyer, Allied Irish Banks plc; Benjamin Orazem, SRC d.o.o.; Sue Shaw, TriCentrica; Marco Smith, iCore Ltd; Hon P Suen, ECT Service Ltd; and Paul Wigzel, Paul Wigzel Training and Consultancy.

1 Introduction

This key element guide is intended to provide a summary of the basic concepts and practice elements of *ITIL Service Design*, which forms part of the core ITIL publication suite.

ITIL is a set of best-practice publications for IT service management (ITSM).[1] ITIL provides guidance on the provision of quality IT services, and on the capabilities needed to support them. ITIL is not a standard that has to be followed; it is guidance that should be read and understood, and used to create value for the service provider and its customers. Organizations are encouraged to adopt ITIL best practices and to adapt them to work in their specific environments in ways that meet their needs.

ITIL is the most widely recognized framework for ITSM in the world. In the 20 years since it was created, ITIL has evolved and changed its breadth and depth as technologies and business practices have developed.

The section numbering in this key element guide is not the same as the section numbers in the core publication, *ITIL Service Design*. Therefore, do not try to use references to section numbers in the core publication when referencing material in this key element guide.

1.1 THE ITIL SERVICE LIFECYCLE

The ITIL framework is based on five stages of the service lifecycle as shown in Figure 1.1, with a core publication providing best-practice guidance for each stage. This guidance includes

---

[1] ITSM and other concepts from this chapter are described in more detail in Chapter 2.

Figure 1.1 The ITIL service lifecycle

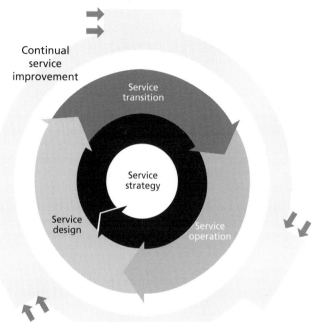

principles, processes and activities, organization and roles, technology, challenges, critical success factors, and risks. The service lifecycle uses a hub-and-spoke design, with service strategy at the hub, and service design, service transition and service operation as the revolving lifecycle stages or 'spokes'. Continual service improvement surrounds and supports all stages of the service lifecycle. Each stage of the lifecycle exerts influence on the others and relies on them for inputs and feedback. In this way, a constant set of checks and balances ensures that as business demand changes, the services can adapt and respond effectively.

In addition to the core publications, there is also a complementary set of ITIL publications providing guidance specific to industry sectors, organization types, operating models and technology architectures.

The following key characteristics of ITIL contribute to its global success:

- **Vendor-neutral** ITIL service management practices are not based on any particular technology platform or industry type. ITIL is owned by the UK government and is not tied to any commercial proprietary practice or solution.
- **Non-prescriptive** ITIL offers robust, mature and time-tested practices that have applicability to all types of service organization. It continues to be useful and relevant in public and private sectors, internal and external service providers, small, medium and large enterprises, and within any technical environment.
- **Best practice** ITIL represents the learning experiences and thought leadership of the world's best-in-class service providers.

1.2 SERVICE DESIGN – KEY ELEMENT GUIDE

ITIL Service Design provides best-practice guidance for the service design stage of the ITIL service lifecycle.

1.2.1   Purpose and objectives of service design

The purpose of the service design stage is to design IT services, together with the governing IT practices, processes and policies, to realize the service provider's strategy and to facilitate the introduction of these services into supported environments, ensuring quality service delivery, customer satisfaction and cost-effective service provision.

The objective of service design is to design IT services so effectively that minimal improvement during their lifecycle will be required. However, continual improvement should be embedded in all service design activities to ensure that the solutions and designs become even more effective over time, and to identify changing business trends that may offer improvement opportunities.

1.2.2   Scope

ITIL Service Design provides guidance for the design of appropriate and innovative IT services to meet current and future agreed business requirements. It describes the principles of service design and looks at identifying, defining and aligning the IT solution with the business requirement. The core publication covers the methods and practices to achieve excellence in service design. It discusses the fundamentals of the design processes and attends to what are called the 'five aspects of service design'.

ITIL Service Design enforces the principle that the initial service design should be driven by a number of factors, including the functional requirements, the requirements within service level agreements (SLAs), the business benefits and the overall design constraints.

The processes considered important to successful service design are design coordination, service catalogue management, service level management, availability management, capacity management, IT service continuity management, information security management and supplier management. It should be noted that almost all of these processes are also active throughout the other stages of the service lifecycle. Other processes are described in detail in the other core ITIL publications. All processes within the service lifecycle must be linked closely together for managing, designing, supporting and maintaining the services, the IT infrastructure, the environment, the applications and the data.

1.2.3   Value to business

Selecting and adopting the best practice as recommended in this publication will assist organizations in delivering significant benefits. With good service design, it is possible to deliver quality, cost-effective services and to ensure that business requirements are consistently met.

Adopting and implementing standard and consistent approaches for service design will:

- **Reduce total cost of ownership (TCO)**   Cost of ownership can only be minimized if all aspects of services, processes and technology are designed properly and implemented as designed.
- **Improve quality of service**   Both service and operational quality will be enhanced through services that are better designed to meet the required outcomes of the customer.
- **Ease the implementation of new or changed services** Integrated and full service designs and the production of comprehensive service design packages will support effective and efficient transitions.

- **Improve service alignment**   Involvement of service design from the conception of the service will ensure that new or changed services match business needs, with services designed to meet service level requirements.
- **Improve effectiveness of service management and IT processes**   Processes will be designed with optimal quality and cost effectiveness.

1.3   CONTEXT

Each core ITIL publication addresses those capabilities that have a direct impact on a service provider's performance. The core is expected to provide structure, stability and strength to service management capabilities, with durable principles, methods and tools. This serves to protect investments and provide the necessary basis for measurement, learning and improvement.

1.3.1   Service strategy

At the centre of the service lifecycle is service strategy. Value creation begins here with understanding organizational objectives and customer needs. Every organizational asset, including people, processes and products, should support the strategy.

ITIL Service Strategy provides guidance on how to view service management not only as an organizational capability but as a strategic asset. It describes the principles underpinning the practice of service management which are useful for developing service management policies, guidelines and processes across the service lifecycle.

Organizations already practising ITIL can use *ITIL Service Strategy* to guide a strategic review of their service management capabilities and to improve the alignment between those capabilities and their business strategies. *ITIL Service Strategy* will encourage readers to stop and think about *why* something is to be done before thinking of *how*.

1.3.2   Service design

Service design is the stage in the lifecycle that turns a service strategy into a plan for delivering business objectives. *ITIL Service Design* provides guidance for the design and development of services and service management practices. It covers design principles and methods for converting strategic objectives into portfolios of services and service assets. The scope of *ITIL Service Design* includes the changes and improvements necessary to increase or maintain value to customers over the lifecycle of services, the continuity of services, the achievement of service levels, and conformance to standards and regulations.

1.3.3   Service transition

ITIL Service Transition provides guidance for the development and improvement of capabilities for introducing new and changed services into supported environments. It describes how to transition an organization from one state to another while controlling risk and supporting organizational knowledge for decision support. It ensures that the value(s) identified in the service strategy, and encoded in the service design, are effectively transitioned so that they can be realized in service operation.

1.3.4   Service operation

ITIL Service Operation describes best practice for managing services in supported environments. It includes guidance on achieving effectiveness and efficiency in the delivery and support of services to ensure value for the customer, the users and the service provider. *ITIL Service Operation* provides guidance on how to maintain stability in service operation, even while allowing for changes in design, scale, scope and service levels.

1.3.5 Continual service improvement

ITIL Continual Service Improvement provides guidance on creating and maintaining value for customers through better strategy, design, transition and operation of services. It combines principles, practices and methods from quality management, change management and capability improvement.

ITIL Continual Service Improvement describes best practice for achieving incremental and large-scale improvements in service quality, operational efficiency and business continuity, and for ensuring that the service portfolio continues to be aligned to business needs.

2 Service management as a practice

2.1 SERVICES AND SERVICE MANAGEMENT

2.1.1 Services

Definitions

Service: A means of delivering value to customers by facilitating outcomes customers want to achieve without the ownership of specific costs and risks.

IT service: A service provided by an IT service provider. An IT service is made up of a combination of information technology, people and processes. A customer-facing IT service directly supports the business processes of one or more customers and its service level targets should be defined in a service level agreement. Other IT services, called supporting services, are not directly used by the business but are required by the service provider to deliver customer-facing services.

Outcome: The result of carrying out an activity, following a process, or delivering an IT service etc. The term is used to refer to intended results, as well as to actual results.

An outcome-based definition of service moves IT organizations beyond business–IT alignment towards business–IT integration. Customers seek outcomes but do not wish to have accountability or ownership of all the associated costs and risks. The customer can judge the value of a service based on a comparison of cost or price and reliability with the desired outcome. Customer satisfaction is also important. Customer expectations keep shifting, and a service provider that does not track this will soon lose business.

2.1.2   Service management

Business would like IT services to behave like other utilities such as water, electricity or the telephone. Simply having the best technology does not ensure that the IT service will provide utility-like reliability. Service management can bring this utility quality of service to the business.

> **Definitions**
>
> *Service management*: A set of specialized organizational capabilities for providing value to customers in the form of services.
>
> *Service provider*: An organization supplying services to one or more internal or external customers.

The more mature a service provider's capabilities are, the greater is their ability to meet the needs of the customer. The act of transforming capabilities and resources into valuable services is at the core of service management. The origins of service management are in traditional service businesses such as airlines, banks and hotels.

2.1.3   IT service management

Every IT organization should act as a service provider, using service management to ensure that they deliver outcomes required by their customers. A service level agreement (SLA) is used to document agreements between an IT service provider and a customer. An SLA describes the service, documents targets, and specifies the responsibilities of the service provider and the customer.

2.1.4 Service providers

There are three main types of service provider:

- **Type I – internal service provider**   This type is embedded within a business unit. There may be several Type I service providers within an organization.
- **Type II – shared services unit**   An internal service provider that provides shared IT services to more than one business unit.
- **Type III – external service provider**   A service provider that provides IT services to external customers.

IT service management (ITSM) concepts are often described in the context of only one of these types. In reality most organizations have a combination of IT service provider types.

2.1.5 Stakeholders in service management

Stakeholders have an interest in an organization, project or service etc. and may also be interested in the activities, targets, resources or deliverables. There are many stakeholders inside the service provider. There are also many external stakeholders, for example:

- **Customers**   Those who buy goods or services. Customers define and agree the service level targets.
- **Users**   Those who use the service on a day-to-day basis.
- **Suppliers**   Third parties responsible for supplying goods or services that are required to deliver IT services.

There is a difference between internal customers and external customers:

- **Internal customers**   These work for the same business as the service provider – for example, the marketing department uses IT services.

■ **External customers** These work for a different business from the service provider. External customers typically purchase services by means of a legally binding contract or agreement.

2.1.6 Utility and warranty

From the customer's perspective, value consists of achieving business objectives. The value of a service is created by combining utility (fitness for purpose) and warranty (fitness for use).

■ **Utility** is the ability to meet a particular need. It is often described as 'what the service does' – for example, a service that enables a business unit to process orders.
■ **Warranty** is an assurance that the service will meet its agreed requirements. Warranty includes the ability of a service to be available when needed, to provide the required capacity, and to provide the required reliability in terms of continuity and security.

The value of a service is only created when both utility and warranty are designed and delivered.

Information about the desired business outcomes, opportunities, customers, utility and warranty of the service is used to develop the definition of a service. Using an outcome-based definition helps to ensure that managers plan and execute all aspects of service management from the customer's perspective.

2.1.7 Best practices in the public domain

Organizations benchmark themselves against peers and seek to close gaps in capabilities. This enables them to become more competitive. One way to close gaps is the adoption of best practices. There are several sources for best practice including public frameworks, standards and the proprietary knowledge of organizations and individuals. ITIL is the most widely recognized and trusted source of best-practice guidance for ITSM.

2.2 BASIC CONCEPTS

2.2.1 Assets, resources and capabilities

The relationship between service providers and customers revolves around the use of assets – both those of the service provider and those of the customer. The performance of customer assets is a primary concern for service management.

> **Definitions**
>
> *Asset*: Any resource or capability.
>
> *Customer asset*: Any resource or capability used by a customer to achieve a business outcome.
>
> *Service asset*: Any resource or capability used by a service provider to deliver services to a customer.

There are two types of asset – resources and capabilities. Resources are direct inputs for production. Capabilities represent an organization's ability to coordinate, control and deploy resources to produce value. It is relatively easy to acquire resources compared to capabilities. Figure 2.1 shows examples of capabilities and resources.

Figure 2.1 Examples of capabilities and resources

Capabilities	Resources
Management	Financial capital
Organization	Infrastructure
Processes	Applications
Knowledge	Information
People (experience, skills and relationships)	People (number of employees)

2.2.2 Processes

Definition: process

A process is a structured set of activities designed to accomplish a specific objective. A process takes one or more defined inputs and turns them into defined outputs.

Process characteristics include:

■ **Measurability**   We can measure the process in a relevant manner.

- **Specific results**   The process delivers specific results, which must be individually identifiable and countable.
- **Customers**   The process delivers its primary results to a customer or stakeholder. Customers may be internal or external to the organization.
- **Responsiveness to specific triggers**   The process should be traceable to a specific trigger.

The outputs from the process should be driven by the process objectives. Process measurement and metrics can be built into the process to control and improve the process as illustrated in Figure 2.2.

Figure 2.2 Process model

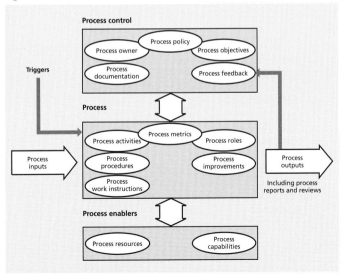

2.2.3 Organizing for service management

Best practices described in ITIL need to be tailored to
suit organizations and situations. The starting point for
organizational design is service strategy.

2.2.3.1 Functions

A function is a team or group of people and the tools or
other resources they use to carry out one or more processes
or activities. In larger organizations, a function may be
performed by several departments, teams and groups. In smaller
organizations, one person or group can perform multiple
functions – for example, a technical management department
could also incorporate the service desk function.

ITIL Service Operation describes the following functions:

- **Service desk** The single point of contact for users. A typical
  service desk manages incidents and service requests, and also
  handles communication with the users.
- **Technical management** Provides technical skills and
  resources needed to manage the IT infrastructure throughout
  the service lifecycle.
- **IT operations management** Executes the daily operational
  activities needed to manage IT services and the supporting IT
  infrastructure.
- **Application management** Is responsible for managing
  applications throughout their lifecycle. This differs from
  application development which is mainly concerned with
  one-time activities for requirements, design and build of
  applications.

The other core ITIL publications rely on the technical and
application management functions described in *ITIL Service*

Operation, but they do not define any additional functions in detail.

2.2.3.2 Roles

The core ITIL publications provide guidelines and examples of role descriptions. In many cases roles will need to be combined or separated.

> **Definition: role**
>
> A role is a set of responsibilities, activities and authorities granted to a person or team. A role is defined in a process or function. One person or team may have multiple roles – for example, the roles of configuration manager and change manager may be carried out by a single person.

Roles are often confused with job titles but they are not the same. Each organization defines job titles and job descriptions, and individuals holding these job titles can perform one or more roles. See Chapter 5 for more details about roles and responsibilities.

2.2.4 The service portfolio

The service portfolio is the complete set of services managed by a service provider, and it represents the service provider's commitments and investments across all customers and market spaces. It consists of three parts:

- **Service pipeline** Services that are under consideration or development, but are not yet available to customers. The service pipeline is a service provider's business view of possible future services.

■ **Service catalogue**   Live IT services, including those available for deployment. It is the only part of the service portfolio that is published to customers. It includes a customer-facing view (or views) of the IT services. It also includes information about supporting services required by the service provider.
■ **Retired services**   Services that have retired.

Service providers often find it useful to distinguish customer-facing services from supporting services:

■ **Customer-facing services** are visible to the customer. These normally support the customer's business processes and facilitate outcomes desired by the customer.
■ **Supporting services** support or 'underpin' the customer-facing services. These are typically invisible to the customer, but are essential to the delivery of customer-facing services.

Figure 2.3 The service portfolio and its contents

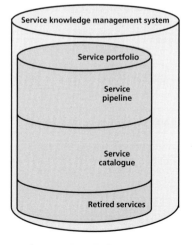

Figure 2.3 illustrates the components of the service portfolio. These are important components of the service knowledge management system (SKMS) described in section 2.2.5.

2.2.5 Knowledge management and the SKMS

Knowledge and information enable people to perform activities and support information flow between lifecycle stages and processes. Implementing knowledge management enables effective decision support and reduces risks.

ITIL Service Transition describes an architecture for a service knowledge management system (SKMS) with four layers:

- **Presentation layer** Enables searching, browsing, retrieving, updating, subscribing and collaboration. Different views are provided for different audiences.
- **Knowledge-processing layer** Where information is converted into knowledge which enables decision-making.
- **Information integration layer** Provides integrated information from data in multiple sources in the data layer.
- **Data layer** Includes tools for data discovery and collection, and data items in unstructured and structured forms.

2.3 GOVERNANCE AND MANAGEMENT SYSTEMS

2.3.1 Governance

Governance defines the common directions, policies and rules that both the business and IT use to conduct business.

> **Definition: governance**
>
> Ensures that policies and strategy are actually implemented, and that required processes are correctly followed. Governance includes defining roles and responsibilities, measuring and reporting, and taking actions to resolve any issues identified.

Governance applies a consistently managed approach at all levels of the organization by ensuring a clear strategy is set, and by defining the policies needed to achieve the strategy.

2.3.2 Management systems

Many businesses have adopted management system standards for competitive advantage, to ensure a consistent approach in implementing service management, and to support governance.

An organization can adopt multiple management system standards, such as:

- A quality management system (ISO 9001)
- An environmental management system (ISO 14000)
- A service management system (ISO/IEC 20000)
- An information security management system (ISO/IEC 27001)
- A management system for software asset management (ISO/IEC 19770).

As there are common elements between such management systems, they should be managed in an integrated way rather than having separate management systems.

ISO management system standards use the Plan-Do-Check-Act (PDCA) cycle shown in Figure 2.4. This PDCA cycle is used in each of the core ITIL publications.

> **Definition: ISO/IEC 20000**
> An international standard for IT service management.

ISO/IEC 20000 is an international standard that allows organizations to prove best practice in ITSM. Part 1 specifies requirements for the service provider to plan, establish, implement, operate, monitor, review, maintain and improve a

Figure 2.4 Plan-Do-Check-Act cycle

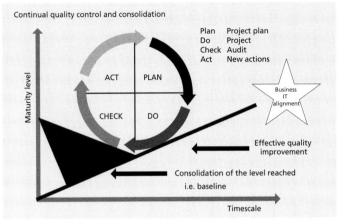

Continual quality control and consolidation

Plan	Project plan
Do	Project
Check	Audit
Act	New actions

Maturity level

ACT   PLAN

CHECK   DO

Business IT alignment

Effective quality improvement

Consolidation of the level reached i.e. baseline

Timescale

service management system (SMS). One of the most common routes for an organization to achieve the requirements of ISO/IEC 20000 is by adopting ITIL.

2.4   THE SERVICE LIFECYCLE

The service lifecycle is an organizing framework, supported by the organizational structure, service portfolio and service models within an organization. See Chapter 1 for an introduction to each ITIL service lifecycle stage.

2.4.1   Specialization and coordination across the lifecycle

Organizations should function in the same manner as a high-performing sports team. Each player in a team and each member of the team's organization who are not players position themselves to support the goal of the team. Each player and team member has a different specialization that contributes to the whole. The team matures over time taking into account feedback from experience, best practice and current processes and procedures to become an agile high-performing team.

Specialization allows for expert focus on components of the service but components of the service also need to work together for value. Coordination across the lifecycle creates an environment focused on business and customer outcomes instead of just IT objectives and projects. Specialization combined with coordination helps to manage expertise, improve focus and reduce overlaps and gaps in processes.

Adopting technology to automate the processes and provide management information that supports the processes is also important for effective and efficient service management.

2.4.2   Processes through the service lifecycle

Each core ITIL publication includes guidance on service management processes as shown in Table 2.1.

Most ITIL roles, processes and functions have activities that take place across multiple stages of the service lifecycle. For example:

- Service validation and testing may design tests during the service design stage and perform these tests during service transition.
- Technical management provides input to strategic decisions about technology, and assists in the design and transition of infrastructure.
- Business relationship managers assist in gathering requirements during the service design stage of the lifecycle, and take part in the management of major incidents during the service operation stage.

Table 2.1 The processes described in each core ITIL publication

Core ITIL lifecycle publication	Processes described in the publication
ITIL Service Strategy	Strategy management for IT services
	Service portfolio management
	Financial management for IT services
	Demand management
	Business relationship management
ITIL Service Design	Design coordination
	Service catalogue management
	Service level management
	Availability management
	Capacity management
	IT service continuity management
	Information security management
	Supplier management
ITIL Service Transition	Transition planning and support
	Change management
	Service asset and configuration management
	Release and deployment management
	Service validation and testing
	Change evaluation
	Knowledge management

Table continues

Table 2.1 *continued*

Core ITIL lifecycle publication	Processes described in the publication
ITIL Service Operation	Event management
	Incident management
	Request fulfilment
	Problem management
	Access management
ITIL Continual Service Improvement	Seven-step improvement process

The strength of the service lifecycle relies on continual feedback throughout each stage of the lifecycle. At every point in the service lifecycle, monitoring, assessment and feedback drives decisions about the need for minor course corrections or major service improvement initiatives.

3 Service design principles

The main purpose of the service design stage of the lifecycle is the design of new or changed services for introduction into the live environment. The retirement of a service also constitutes a 'change' and must be carefully designed. This stage of the lifecycle is also responsible for the design of the service provider's overall service management system and the many aspects required to deliver services effectively.

3.1 SERVICE DESIGN BASICS

All designs and design activities need to be driven principally by the business needs and requirements of the organization. Adopting and implementing standardized and consistent approaches for service design will:

- Enable accurate estimation of the cost, timing, resource requirement and risks associated with service design
- Result in higher volumes of successful change
- Make design methods easier for people to adopt and follow
- Enable service design assets to be shared and reused across projects and services
- Reduce delays resulting from the need to redesign prior to completion of service transition
- Improve expectation management of all stakeholders
- Ensure that new or changed services will be maintainable and cost-effective.

The key output of the service design stage is the design of service solutions to meet the changing requirements of the business. It is important that a holistic, results-driven approach to all aspects of design is adopted, and that when changing any of the individual elements of design all other aspects are considered.

Not every change within an IT service will require the same level of service design activity. Every change, no matter how small, needs to be designed, but the scale of the activity necessary to ensure success varies greatly from one change type to another. All changes should be assessed for their service design requirements to determine the correct activities to undertake in each circumstance.

3.1.1   IT service design and overall business change

IT service design is a part of the overall business change process. This is illustrated in Figure 3.1. The element changing on the business side is most often a business process (a 'business process change'), resulting in the need for a supporting change in IT service.

The role of the service design stage within this overall business change process can be described as the design of appropriate and innovative IT services, including their architectures, processes, policies and documentation, to meet current and future agreed business requirements.

Figure 3.1 The business change process

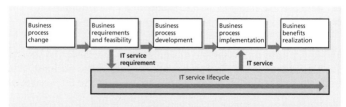

3.1.2   Service design scope and flow

The service design stage of the lifecycle starts with new or changed business requirements and ends with the development of a service solution designed to meet the documented needs of the business. This solution, together with its service design package (SDP), is then passed to service transition.

There are five aspects of service design which must all be considered together:

- **Service solutions for new or changed services**   The requirements for new or changed services are identified, analysed, documented and agreed, and a solution design is produced that fulfils the requirements and conforms to constraints, policies and standards.
- **The management information systems and tools**   These should be reviewed to ensure that they are capable of supporting the new or changed service.
- **The technology architectures and management architectures** These are reviewed to ensure that all the technology architectures and management architectures are consistent with the new or changed service and have the capability to operate, support and maintain the new service.
- **The processes required**   These are reviewed to ensure that the processes, roles, responsibilities and skills have the capability to operate, support and maintain the new or changed service. This includes all IT and service management processes, not just the processes involved in the service design stage itself.
- **The measurement methods and metrics**   These are reviewed to ensure that the existing measurement methods can provide the required metrics on the new or changed service.

Greater detail on these aspects may be found in section 3.7.

Service design activities should focus on the business processes supported and business value provided, and ensure that the ability to measure and demonstrate value to the business is incorporated in all aspects of service design.

3.1.3   Comprehensive and integrated service designs

It is essential that IT systems and services are designed, planned, implemented and managed appropriately for the business as a whole. The implementation of ITSM as a practice is about preparing and planning the effective and efficient use of the four Ps of service design: the people, the processes, the products (services, technology and tools) and the partners (suppliers, manufacturers and vendors), as illustrated in Figure 3.2.

The design activities must not just consider each of the components of a service in isolation, but also must consider the relationships between the components (and their interactions

Figure 3.2 The four Ps of service design

People

Processes

Products/
technology

Partners/
suppliers

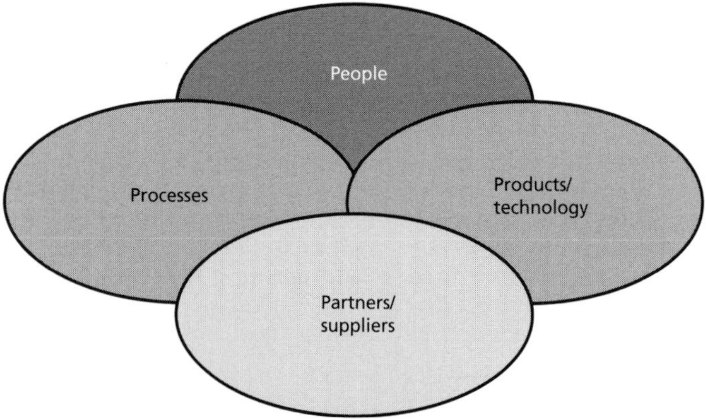

with and dependencies on other components and services) to provide an effective and comprehensive solution that meets the business needs.

Many companies have a committee consisting of senior management from the business and IT, possibly referred to as the IT strategy or steering group (ISG). This committee has overall accountability for setting governance, direction, policy and strategy for IT services which form a critical element of the overall service management system of the service provider.

3.2 SERVICE DESIGN GOALS

The main goals and objectives of service design are to:

- Design services to satisfy business objectives and align with business needs, by coordinating all design activities for IT services
- Design services that can be easily and efficiently developed and enhanced within appropriate timescales and costs, and minimize the long-term costs of service provision
- Design an efficient and effective service management system, including processes for the design, transition, operation and improvement of high-quality IT services, together with the supporting tools, systems and information
- Assist in the development of policies and standards in all areas of design and planning of IT services and processes
- Contribute to the improvement of the overall quality of IT service within the imposed design constraints.

3.3 BALANCED DESIGN

The design of services requires a balance, ensuring that both the functional requirements and the performance targets are met.

All requirements must be balanced with regard to resources available, the required timescale and costs. In the search for this balance, we are concerned with three things:

- **Functionality**   The service or product and everything that is part of the service and its provision
- **Resources**   The people, technology and money available
- **Schedule**   The timescales for completion.

3.4   IDENTIFYING SERVICE REQUIREMENTS

Service design must consider all elements of the service. This approach should assess the service and its components and their interrelationships, ensuring that the services delivered meet the requirements of the business in all areas:

- Scalability to meet future requirements
- The business processes and business units supported by the service
- The agreed business requirements for functionality (i.e. utility)
- The service level requirements (SLR) or SLA (addressing warranty)
- The technology components used to deploy and deliver the service
- The supporting services and components and their associated operational level agreements (OLAs) and underpinning contracts
- The performance measurements and metrics required.

3.5   IDENTIFYING AND DOCUMENTING BUSINESS REQUIREMENTS AND DRIVERS

IT must retain accurate information on business requirements and drivers. This requires IT to develop and maintain close, regular and appropriate relationships and exchange of information in order to understand the operational, tactical and strategic requirements of the business. The business relationship management process as detailed in *ITIL Service Strategy* plays a vital role in this work. The business information needs to be obtained and agreed in three main areas to maintain service alignment:

- Information on the requirements for existing services
- Information on the requirements for new services
- Information on the requirements for retiring services.

3.6   DESIGN ACTIVITIES

The inputs to design activities are:

- Business, IT and service management vision, strategies, objectives, policies and plans
- Details of business requirements, including requirements for compliance with standards and regulations
- All constraints and budgets
- The service portfolio
- ITSM processes, risks and issues registers, and improvement registers
- Service management plans, including service level management plans, SLAs and SLRs, service improvement plan(s) (SIPs), capacity plans, availability plans and IT service continuity plans.

The key deliverables from the design activities are:

- Designs for new or changed services, processes and technologies, including sourcing strategy (buy or build or a combination of both approaches), documented in service design packages

■ Process review and analysis reports, with designs for revised and improved processes and procedures
■ Revised designs, plans and technology and management architectures
■ Designs for revised measurement methods
■ Revised budgets and service costing.

3.7 DESIGN ASPECTS

The five aspects of service design are listed in section 3.1.2.

3.7.1 Designing service solutions

A formal and structured approach is required to produce the service at the right cost, utility (functionality) and warranty and within the right time frame.

The key areas that need to be considered within the design of the service solution include:

■ Analysing agreed business requirements
■ Reviewing existing IT services and infrastructure and producing alternative service solutions, with a view to reusing or exploiting existing components and services wherever possible
■ Designing the service solution to the new requirements, including constituent components, and documenting this design including clear service acceptance criteria (SAC)
■ Agreeing the preferred solution and its planned outcomes and targets (utility and warranty) and ensuring that it is in balance with all corporate and IT strategies, policies, plans and architectural documents
■ Assembling an SDP for the subsequent transition, operation and improvement of the new or changed service solution.

3.7.2   Designing management information systems and tools

The most effective way of managing all aspects of services through their lifecycle is by using appropriate management information systems and tools to support and automate efficient processes. Management information systems are typically part of a larger system or framework of policies, processes, functions, standards, guidelines and tools that are planned and managed together and used to ensure that the desired objectives are achieved. This larger system or framework is known as a management system; examples include a quality management system, an information security management system, or even the overall service management system.

The service portfolio is the most critical management information system used to support all processes. It describes services in terms of business value. It articulates business needs and the provider's response to those needs. It should contain information about every service, regardless of status, and be designed to meet the needs of all those who use it. Ideally, the service portfolio should form part of a comprehensive SKMS and be registered in the configuration management system (CMS).

3.7.3   Designing technology architectures and management architectures

The architectural design activities within an IT organization are concerned with providing the overall strategic blueprints for the development and deployment of an IT infrastructure that will satisfy current and future needs of the business.

The 'architecture' can be described as the fundamental organization of a system, embodied in its components, their relationships to each other and to the environment, and the principles guiding its design and evolution. 'System' is used in the most general sense to mean a collection of components organized to accomplish a specific function or set of functions.

'Architectural design' is the development and maintenance of IT policies, strategies, architectures, designs, documents, plans and processes for the deployment and subsequent operation and improvement of appropriate IT services and solutions throughout an organization.

The enterprise architecture should show how all elements are integrated in order to achieve the business objectives, and is an essential part of the business architecture. It should include the major areas shown in Figure 3.3.

3.7.4   Designing processes

Once defined, processes should be documented and controlled. Once under control, they can be repeated and become manageable. Degrees of control over processes can be defined, and then process measurement and metrics can be built into the process to control and improve the process.

In the beginning and throughout the process, data enters, is processed, is output and the outcome is measured and reviewed. A process is always organized around a set of objectives. The main outputs from the process should be driven by the objectives and should always include process measurements (metrics), reports and process improvement.

Each organization should adopt a formalized approach to the design and implementation of service management processes. The objective should be to design practical and appropriate processes with 'in-built' improvement mechanisms, so that the effectiveness and efficiency of the processes are improved in the most suitable manner for the organization. Documentation standards, processes and templates should be used to

Figure 3.3 Architectural relationships

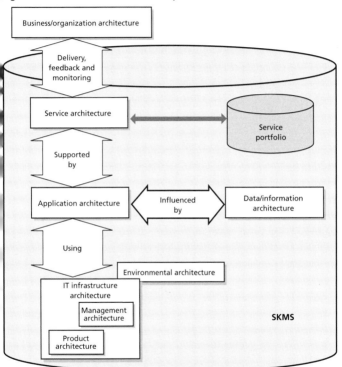

ensure that the processes are easily adopted throughout the organization.

When designing a service or a process, it is imperative that all the roles are clearly defined. To help with this task the RACI model or 'authority matrix' is often used to define the roles and responsibilities in relation to processes and activities. See section 5.2 of this publication for an explanation of the RACI model.

3.7.5   Designing measurement methods and metrics

In order to manage and control processes and services, they have to be monitored and measured. The design of the measurement methods and metrics includes developing metrics to manage and control design activities themselves. Measurements and metrics are covered in detail in *ITIL Continual Service Improvement*.

Care should be exercised when selecting measurements and metrics and the methods used to produce them. All measurements should encourage progression towards meeting business objectives or desired behavioural change.

The process measurements selected should be appropriate for the capability and maturity of the processes being measured and should develop and change as the maturity and capability of the process evolves. There are four types of metrics that can be used:

- **Progress**   Milestones and deliverables in the capability of the process
- **Compliance**   The degree to which the process conforms to governance and regulatory requirements, and the extent to which people comply with the correct use of the process
- **Effectiveness**   The accuracy and correctness of the process and its ability to deliver the 'right result'
- **Efficiency**   The productivity of the process, its speed, throughput and resource utilization.

It is important to aggregate measurements from individual areas, otherwise the following problems could arise:

- Measurements are not aligned with business objectives and needs

■ Decisions and improvement actions are based on incomplete or inaccurate information.

3.8   THE SUBSEQUENT DESIGN ACTIVITIES

Once the service solution has been designed, then subsequent activities must be completed in the service design stage before the solution passes into the service transition stage. These activities relate to the evaluation of alternatives when external suppliers are involved; procurement from selected suppliers; and the development of the service solution. In this context 'development' means the translation of the service design into a plan for the development, reuse or redevelopment of the components required to deliver the service, and the subsequent implementation of the developed service.

3.9   DESIGN CONSTRAINTS

All design activities operate within many constraints which come from the business and service strategy and cover many different areas, as illustrated in Figure 3.4.

The primary constraints that determine the boundaries of a service solution design are the utility and warranty desired by the customer. The service provider will attempt to fulfil everything requested by the customer in these areas, but other constraints may result in compromises. The designer can only provide a solution that fits within the currently known constraints, or perhaps renegotiate some of the constraints – for instance, by obtaining a bigger budget.

Figure 3.4 Design constraints driven by strategy

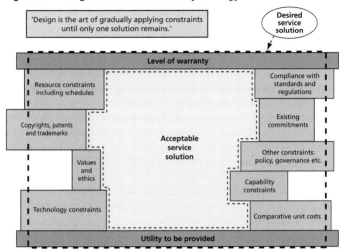

3.10 SERVICE DESIGN MODELS

The model selected for the design of IT services will depend mainly on the model selected for their delivery. Before adopting a design model for a major new service, a review of the current capability and provisions with respect to all aspects of the delivery of IT services should be conducted.

There are many different delivery strategies or models that can be used, reflecting how and to what degree the service provider will rely on suppliers. Table 3.1 briefly describes the main categories of sourcing structure (delivery strategy). Delivery practices tend to fall into one of these categories or some variant of them.

Table 3.1 Main sourcing structures (delivery strategies)

Sourcing structure	Description
Insourcing	Uses internal organizational resources.
Outsourcing	Utilizes the resources of an external organization or organizations in a formal arrangement to provide a well-defined portion of a service's lifecycle.
Co-sourcing or multi-sourcing	Often a combination of insourcing and outsourcing, using a number of organizations working together to co-source key elements within the lifecycle.
Partnership	Formal arrangements between two or more organizations to work together. The focus tends to be on strategic partnerships that leverage critical expertise or market opportunities.
Business process outsourcing (BPO)	Relocating entire business functions using formal arrangements where one organization provides and manages the other organization's entire business process(es) or function(s) in a low-cost location.
Application service provision	Arrangements with an application service provider (ASP) organization to provide shared computer-based services over a network from the service provider's premises.

Table continues

Table 3.1 *continued*

Sourcing structure	Description
Knowledge process outsourcing (KPO)	KPO organizations provide domain-based processes and business expertise rather than just process expertise. The organization is not only required to execute a process, but also to make certain low-level decisions based on knowledge of local conditions or industry-specific information.
'Cloud'	Cloud service providers offer specific predefined services, usually on demand. Services are usually standard, but can be customized to suit a specific organization if there is enough demand for the service. Cloud services can be offered internally, but generally refer to outsourced service provision.

3.11   SERVICE DESIGN INPUTS AND OUTPUTS

The main inputs to service design are information and documents that define and describe the strategy, policies, priorities and decisions made during service strategy, as well as feedback and requirements from the other lifecycle stages.

The main output is the service design package, which includes all the information needed to manage the entire lifecycle of the new or changed service, along with change requests and agreements to support delivery of the service.

4 Service design processes

4.1 DESIGN COORDINATION

4.1.1 Purpose and objectives

The purpose of the design coordination process is to ensure that the goals and objectives of the service design stage are met by providing and maintaining a single point of coordination and control for all activities and processes within this stage of the service lifecycle.

The objectives of the design coordination process are to:

- Ensure the consistent design of all of the five aspects of service design to meet current and evolving business outcomes and requirements
- Coordinate all design activities across projects, changes, suppliers and support teams, and manage schedules, resources and conflicts
- Produce service design packages (SDPs) based on service charters and change requests and ensure that they are handed over to service transition
- Improve the effectiveness and efficiency of service design activities and processes.

4.1.2 Scope

The scope of the design coordination process includes all design activity, particularly new or changed service solutions for transition into (or out of) the live environment. Some design efforts will be part of a project, whereas others will be managed through the change process alone without a formally defined project.

4.1.3   Value to business

The main value of the design coordination process is the production of a set of consistent quality solution designs and SDPs that will provide the desired business outcomes.

4.1.4   Policies, principles and basic concepts

The design coordination process provides guidelines and policies to allow for a holistic approach to all design activities and the coordination to ensure that these are followed.

Since not all service designs are of the same type or scope, the service provider should define those policies setting out which particular service design efforts require specific types of attention from design coordination. The level of required documentation should also be established by policy.

Important principles of design coordination include:

- **Balance and prioritization**   The goal is a comprehensive design that addresses all aspects of utility and warranty, as well as the needs of the service throughout its lifecycle. The structure and control of design activities allow for efficient management of the work and improved results.
- **Integration with project management**   As part of design coordination, practices, documents, procedures or deliverables needed for design success should be integrated into the overall project management methodology, and all project managers must be trained to contribute appropriately.

4.1.5   Process activities, methods and techniques

Design coordination activities fall into two categories.

4.1.5.1 Activities relating to the overall service design lifecycle stage

These activities include the development, deployment and continual improvement of service design practices, as well as the coordination of design activity across projects and changes.

4.1.5.2 Activities relating to each individual design

These activities focus on ensuring that each individual design effort and SDP, whether part of a project or simply associated with a change, conforms with defined practices and produces a design that will support the required business outcomes.

4.1.6 Triggers, inputs, outputs and interfaces

The triggers for the design coordination process are changes in business requirements and services. The main triggers are change requests and the creation of new programmes and projects. Another trigger for the review of design coordination activities would be the revision of the overall IT strategy.

Key inputs to the design coordination process include:

- Service charters for new or changed services, change requests, change records and authorized changes
- The service portfolio, including the service catalogue and the business requirements for new or changed services in terms of service packages and service options
- The programme and project schedule
- Feedback from all other processes.

The most important outputs of design coordination are comprehensive and consistent service designs and SDPs.

The principal interfaces are to the adjacent stages of the lifecycle:

- **Service strategy**   Using information contained within the IT strategy and service portfolio
- **Service transition**   With the handover of the design of service solutions within the SDP.

In addition, the design coordination process also interfaces with all the processes that include service design activity, with particular emphasis on interfaces with service level management.

4.1.7   Critical success factors and key performance indicators

Examples of critical success factors (CSFs) and key performance indicators (KPIs) for the design coordination process include:

- **CSF**   Accurate and consistent SDPs
    - **KPI**   Reduction in the number of subsequent revisions of the content of SDPs
    - **KPI**   Percentage reduction in the re-work required for new or changed service solutions in subsequent lifecycle stages
- **CSF**   Managing conflicting demands for shared resources
    - **KPI**   Reduced number of issues caused by conflict for service design resources
    - **KPI**   Percentage increase in the number of successful new and changed services in terms of outcomes, quality, cost and timeliness
    - **KPI**   Improved effectiveness and efficiency in the service design processes, activities and supporting systems.

4.1.8   Challenges and risks

The major challenge facing design coordination is maintaining high-quality designs and SDPs consistently across all areas of the business, services and infrastructure. A related challenge is ensuring that sufficient time and resources are devoted to design coordination and that the roles and responsibilities of the process are assigned to appropriate individuals and/or groups to ensure completion. Another significant challenge is developing common practices that produce the desired high-quality designs without unnecessary bureaucracy.

Risks associated with the design coordination process include:

■ Lack of information on business priorities and impacts
■ Poorly defined requirements and desired outcomes
■ Poor communication
■ Lack of involvement from all relevant stakeholders including customers, users, and support and other operations staff
■ Insufficient interaction with and input from other lifecycle stages.

4.2   SERVICE CATALOGUE MANAGEMENT

4.2.1   Purpose and objectives

The purpose of the service catalogue management process is to provide and maintain a single source of consistent information on all operational services and those being prepared to be run operationally, and to ensure that it is widely available to those who are authorized to access it.

The objectives of the service catalogue management process are to:

■ Ensure that the service catalogue is accurate and reflects the current details, status, interfaces and dependencies of all services that are being run, or being prepared to run, in the live environment, according to the defined policies
■ Ensure that the service catalogue is made available to those approved to access it

■   Ensure that the service catalogue supports the evolving needs of all other service management processes.

4.2.2   Scope

The scope of the service catalogue management process is to provide and maintain accurate information on all services that are being transitioned or have been transitioned to the live environment. The services presented in the service catalogue may be listed individually or, more typically, some or all of the services may be presented in the form of service packages.

4.2.3   Value to business

The service catalogue includes a customer-facing view (or views) of IT services, how they are intended to be used, the business processes they enable, and the levels and quality of service the customer can expect.

Through the work of service catalogue management, organizations can:

■   Ensure a common understanding of IT services and improved relationships between the customer and service provider
■   Improve efficiency and effectiveness of other service management processes
■   Improve knowledge, alignment and focus on the 'business value' of each service throughout the service provider.

4.2.4 Policies, principles and basic concepts

Definition: service catalogue

The service catalogue is a database or structured document with information about all live IT services, including those available for deployment. The service catalogue is published to customers and is used to support the sale and delivery of IT services. It includes information about deliverables, prices, contact points, ordering and request processes.

Each organization should develop and maintain a policy for both the overall service portfolio and the constituent service catalogue, relating to the services recorded and what details are recorded (including what statuses are recorded for each service).

Each organization needs also to develop a policy of what a service is and how it is to be defined and agreed.

The details of this policy will be influenced by many factors, including:

■ Target audiences and anticipated uses for the service catalogue

■ Organizational culture, practices and maturity levels.

4.2.4.1 Different types of service

It may be useful to define a hierarchy of services within the service catalogue, by qualifying exactly what type of service is recorded. The most valuable distinction is between:

■ **Customer-facing services** IT services that are seen by the customer. These support the customer, directly facilitating one or more outcomes desired by them.

■ **Supporting services** IT services that support or 'underpin' customer-facing services. These are typically invisible to the customer, but essential to the delivery of customer-facing IT services.

Supporting services may be of many different types such as infrastructure services, network services, application services or technical services.

Not every service or every piece of information is of interest to every person or group. When service providers have many customers or serve many businesses, there may be multiple service catalogue views projected from the service portfolio.

There is no single correct way to structure and deploy a service catalogue. Each service provider organization will consider its goals, objectives and uses for the service catalogue and create a structure that will meet its needs.

4.2.5 Process activities, methods and techniques

The key activities within the service catalogue management process should include:

4.2.5.1 Service definition

Agreeing and documenting a service definition and description for each service.

4.2.5.2 Interfacing with service portfolio management

Ensuring that the service portfolio and service catalogue are properly aligned and integrated.

4.2.5.3 Service catalogue production

Producing and maintaining an accurate service catalogue, including all interfaces and dependencies with the business and with IT services, supporting services, components and configuration items (CIs).

4.2.6 Triggers, inputs, outputs and interfaces

The triggers for the service catalogue management process are changes in business requirements and services, and therefore one of the main triggers is the change management process. This includes new services, changes to existing services or services being retired.

Inputs to the service catalogue management process include:

■ Business information and IT strategy, plans and financial plans, and information on current and future business requirements
■ Business impact analysis (BIA), CMS and change requests
■ The service portfolio and all related data and documents
■ Feedback from other processes.

The primary output of the service catalogue management process is an accurate and complete service catalogue.

Every service provider process uses the service catalogue, so it could be said that the service catalogue management process interfaces with all processes. The most prominent interfaces include:

■ **Service portfolio management**   This process determines which services will be chartered and eventually enter the service catalogue.
■ **Service asset and configuration management**   This process integrates with service catalogue management to ensure that information in the CMS and information in the service catalogue are appropriately linked.

■ **Service level management**   This process negotiates specific levels of service warranty which will be reflected in the service catalogue.

4.2.7   Critical success factors and key performance indicators

The most important example of a CSF and KPIs for the service catalogue management process are:

■ **CSF**   An accurate service catalogue

- **KPI**   Increase in the number of services recorded and managed within the service catalogue as a percentage of those being delivered and transitioned in the live environment
- **KPI**   Percentage reduction in the number of variances detected between the information contained within the service catalogue and the 'real-world' situation.

4.2.8   Challenges and risks

The major challenge facing service catalogue management is maintaining an accurate service catalogue as part of a service portfolio, incorporating all catalogue views as part of an overall CMS and SKMS.

The risks associated with the provision of an accurate service catalogue are:

■ Inaccuracy or incorrect level of detail of service catalogue data
■ Lack of change control
■ Poor acceptance of the service catalogue and its usage in all operational processes
■ Lack of an up-to-date CMS and SKMS for integration with the service catalogue.

4.3   SERVICE LEVEL MANAGEMENT

4.3.1   Purpose and objectives

The purpose of the service level management (SLM) process is to ensure that all current and planned IT services are delivered to agreed achievable targets. This is accomplished through a constant cycle of negotiating, agreeing, monitoring, reporting on and reviewing IT service targets and achievements, and through instigation of actions to correct or improve the level of service delivered.

The key objectives of SLM are to:

- Define, document, agree, monitor, measure, report and review the level of IT services provided and instigate corrective measures whenever appropriate
- Ensure that specific and measurable targets are developed for all IT services
- Ensure that IT and the customers have a clear and unambiguous expectation of the level of service to be delivered
- Ensure that even when all agreed targets are met, the levels of service delivered are subject to proactive, cost-effective continual improvement.

4.3.2   Scope

The SLM process activity should encompass both existing services and potential future new or changed services. SLM manages the expectation and perception of the business, customers and users and ensures that the quality (warranty) of service delivered is matched to those expectations and needs. To do this effectively, SLM should establish and maintain service level agreements (SLAs) for all live services and manage the level of service provided to meet the targets and quality measurements within the SLAs. SLM should also produce and agree SLRs that document warranty requirements for planned new or changed services.

4.3.3 Value to business

SLM provides a consistent interface to the business for all service-level-related issues. It provides the business with agreed service targets and the required management information to ensure that those targets have been met. When targets are breached, SLM provides feedback on the cause of the breach and details of the actions taken to prevent the breach from recurring.

4.3.4 Policies, principles and basic concepts

An SLA is a written agreement between an IT service provider and their customer(s), defining the key service targets and responsibilities of both parties. It typically defines the warranty a service is to deliver and describes the utility of the service. A partnership should be developed between the IT service provider and the customer, so that a mutually beneficial agreement is reached.

An operational level agreement (OLA) is an agreement between an IT service provider and another part of the same organization that assists with the provision of services.

The service provider should establish policies to define such things as the minimum required content of SLAs and OLAs, when and how agreements are to be reviewed, renewed and/ or renegotiated, and how frequently and using what methods service level reporting will be provided.

When an IT service provider engages a third party to provide goods or services that are needed for the provision of service to their customer(s) it is important that both parties have clear and unambiguous expectations of how the supplier will meet the IT service provider's requirements. This is accomplished by documenting the terms of engagement in an agreement called an 'underpinning contract'. Policy should define how the SLM process contributes to the negotiation of these contracts.

4.3.5 Process activities, methods and techniques

The key activities within the SLM process include:

4.3.5.1 Requirement and target management

Determining, negotiating, documenting and agreeing requirements for new or changed services in SLRs, and managing and reviewing them through the service lifecycle into targets in SLAs for operational services.

4.3.5.2 Performance monitoring

Monitoring and measuring service performance achievements against all targets within SLAs.

4.3.5.3 Service reporting and reviews

Producing service reports and conducting service reviews, identifying improvement opportunities for inclusion in the continual service improvement (CSI) register, and managing SIPs.

4.3.5.4 Agreement negotiation and maintenance

This includes the activity of negotiation, regular review and maintenance of SLAs and OLAs, as well as assisting supplier management in reviewing and revising underpinning contracts or agreements.

SLM must design the most appropriate SLA structure to ensure that all services and all customers are covered in a manner best suited to the organization's needs. Options include:

- **Service-based SLA**   An SLA covering one service, for all the customers of that service. Multiple classes of service (for example, gold, silver and bronze) can be used to increase the effectiveness of service-based SLAs.
- **Customer-based SLA**   An agreement with an individual customer group, covering all the services they use.
- **Multi-level SLAs**   For example, a three-layer structure starting with a generic corporate level SLA, supplemented by customer-based and service-based SLAs.

Other important SLM methods and techniques include:

- Use of clear and concise language in SLAs so that there is no room for ambiguity
- Determining initial targets based on customer SLRs and then working to determine if they can be achieved
- Ensuring that targets in SLAs are supported by achievable targets in associated OLAs and/or underpinning contracts
- Ensuring that all targets in SLAs are measurable
- Holding regular service review meetings with customers to review service achievements, discuss any shortfalls or breaches and define and agree improvement actions.

4.3.6   Triggers, inputs, outputs and interfaces

Triggers that instigate SLM activity include:

- Changes in the service portfolio
- New or changed agreements, SLRs, SLAs, OLAs or contracts
- Service breaches or threatened breaches.

Inputs to the SLM process include:

- Business information about current and future requirements
- Business impact analysis providing information on the impact, priority, risk and number of users associated with each service
- The service portfolio and service catalogue
- Customer and user feedback, complaints and compliments
- Feedback from other processes, together with existing SLAs, SLRs and OLAs and past service reports.

The outputs of SLM should include:

- SLAs and OLAs
- Service reports, review meeting minutes and actions
- Service improvement opportunities
- Revised requirements for underpinning contracts: changes to SLAs or new SLRs may require underpinning contracts to be altered or new contracts to be negotiated and agreed.

The most critical interfaces for the SLM process include:

- **Business relationship management**   Ensures that SLM has a full understanding of the business's needs and priorities and that customers are appropriately involved/represented in SLM
- **Supplier management**   Integrates with SLM to define, negotiate, document and agree terms of service with suppliers to support commitments made in SLAs
- **Availability, capacity, IT service continuity and information security management**   Help to define service level targets and to validate that the targets are realistic
- **Design coordination**   Ensures that the overall service design activities are completed successfully, including SLM's design activities.

4.3.7   Critical success factors and key performance indicators

Examples of CSFs and KPIs for the service level management process include:

- ■ **CSF**   Managing the overall quality of IT services
  - – **KPI**   Percentage reduction in SLA targets threatened
  - – **KPI**   Percentage increase in customer perception and satisfaction of SLA achievements
  - – **KPI**   Percentage reduction in SLA breaches caused as a result of third-party support contracts (underpinning contracts) or internal OLAs
- ■ **CSF**   Deliver the service as previously agreed at affordable costs
  - – **KPI**   Total number and percentage increase in fully documented SLAs in place
  - – **KPI**   Percentage increase in SLAs agreed against operational services being run.

4.3.8   Challenges and risks

Challenges to the SLM process include:

- ■ Difficulty in identifying the right customer representatives
- ■ Selecting the correct service(s) with which to start SLM
- ■ Getting access to monitoring and reporting data for evaluating SLA achievements.

Risks to the SLM process include:

- ■ A lack of accurate input, involvement and commitment from the business and customers
- ■ The process becoming too bureaucratic
- ■ Lack of appropriate and up-to-date CMS and SKMS
- ■ Business and customer measurements becoming too difficult to obtain

■ Poor and inappropriate communication with the business and customers.

4.4   AVAILABILITY MANAGEMENT

4.4.1   Purpose and objectives

The purpose of the availability management process is to ensure that the level of availability delivered in all IT services meets the agreed availability needs and/or service level targets in a cost-effective and timely manner. Availability management is concerned with meeting both the current and future availability needs of the business.

The key objectives of availability management are to:

■ Produce and maintain an up-to-date availability plan
■ Provide advice and guidance on all availability-related issues
■ Ensure that service availability achievements meet all their agreed targets by managing service and resource-related availability
■ Assist with the diagnosis and resolution of availability-related incidents and problems
■ Proactively improve the availability of services.

4.4.2   Scope

The scope of the availability management process covers the design, implementation, measurement, management and improvement of IT service and component availability. Availability management commences as soon as the availability requirements for an IT service are clear enough to be articulated. It is an ongoing process, finishing only when the IT service is retired.

4.4.3 Value to business

The availability and reliability of IT services can directly influence customer satisfaction and the reputation of the business. Availability management is essential in ensuring that IT delivers the levels of service availability required by the business to satisfy its business objectives and deliver the quality of service demanded by its customers.

4.4.4 Policies, principles and basic concepts

The service provider organization should establish policies defining when and how availability management must be engaged throughout each lifecycle stage. Policies should also be established regarding the criteria to be used to define availability and unavailability of a service or component and how each will be measured.

Availability management has two inter-connected levels:

■ **Service availability** Involves all aspects of service availability and unavailability and the impact of, or the potential impact of, component unavailability on service availability.
■ **Component availability** Involves all aspects of component availability and unavailability.

Availability management relies on the monitoring, measurement, analysis and reporting of the following aspects.

4.4.4.1 Availability

Availability is the ability of a service, component or configuration item (CI) to perform its agreed function when required. It is often measured and reported as a percentage. Note that downtime should only be included in the calculation when it occurs within the agreed service time (AST).

4.4.4.2   Reliability

Reliability is a measure of how long a service, component or CI can perform its agreed function without interruption. The reliability of the service is often measured and reported as the mean time between service incidents (MTBSI) or mean time between failures (MTBF):

$$\text{Reliability (MTBSI in hours)} = \frac{\text{Available time in hours}}{\text{Number of breaks}}$$

$$\text{Reliability (MTBF in hours)} = \frac{\text{Available time in hours} - \text{Total downtime in hours}}{\text{Number of breaks}}$$

4.4.4.3   Maintainability

Maintainability is a measure of how quickly and effectively a service, component or CI can be restored to normal working after a failure. It is measured and reported as the mean time to restore service (MTRS) and should be calculated using the following formula:

$$\text{Maintainability (MTRS in hours)} = \frac{\text{Total downtime in hours}}{\text{Number of service breaks}}$$

4.4.4.4   Serviceability

Serviceability is the ability of a third-party supplier to meet the terms of its contract. This contract will include agreed levels of availability, reliability and/or maintainability for a supporting service or component.

4.4.4.5 Vital business function

The term vital business function (VBF) is used to reflect the part of a business process that is critical to the success of the business. An IT service may support a number of business functions that are less critical. This distinction is important and should influence availability design and associated costs.

4.4.5 Process activities, methods and techniques

The availability management process includes two key elements:

4.4.5.1 Reactive activities

These involve monitoring, measuring, analysis and management of all events, incidents and problems involving unavailability. These activities are principally performed as part of the operational roles.

4.4.5.2 Proactive activities

These involve proactive planning, design and improvement of availability. These activities are principally performed as part of the design and planning roles.

Availability management reactive and proactive activities are illustrated in Figure 4.1.

In performing availability management, consideration should be given to the following:

■ The most important availability measurements are those that reflect and measure availability from the business and user perspective. The component perspective is not enough.
■ When measuring availability, consider attempting to quantify things such as:
  – Impact by user minutes lost
  – Impact by business transaction.

Figure 4.1 The availability management process

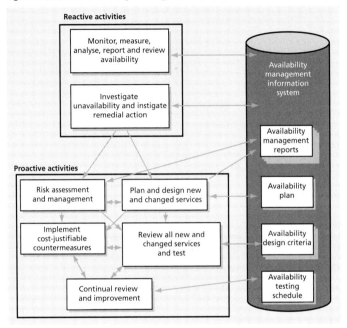

A number of methods and techniques are described in *ITIL Service Design*. Some key examples include:

■ **Unavailability analysis**   All events and incidents causing unavailability of services and components should be investigated, with remedial actions implemented.

Figure 4.2 The expanded incident lifecycle

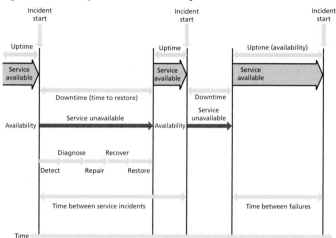

- **The expanded incident lifecycle**   Enables the total IT service downtime for any given incident to be broken down and mapped against the major stages through which all incidents progress (the lifecycle).

  Figure 4.2 illustrates the expanded incident lifecycle.

- **Service failure analysis (SFA)**   A technique providing a structured approach to identifying the underlying causes of service interruptions and recommending improvements to the end-to-end service availability. SFA is essentially a reactive technique.

- **Availability requirements definition**   This includes the identification of VBFs.

- **Designing service for availability**   This ensures that the required level of availability for an IT service can be met. It looks at both the design of the service to meet the business's availability requirements as well as the design points required to resume the service as quickly as possible in the event of a failure.
- **Component failure impact analysis (CFIA)**   A technique used to predict and evaluate the impact on IT services arising from technology component failures, to identify where additional resilience should be considered.

4.4.6   Triggers, inputs, outputs and interfaces

Events that may trigger availability management activity include:

- New or changed business needs or new or changed services
- New or changed SLRs, SLAs, OLAs or contracts
- Service or component breaches, availability events and alerts, including threshold events, exception reports
- Review and revision of designs and strategies.

Key inputs to the availability management process include:

- Business information, business impact information and risk assessments
- Service information from the service portfolio/service catalogue and from the SLM process; also service level targets within SLAs and SLRs, and possibly from the monitoring of SLAs, service reviews and breaches of the SLAs
- Information from other service management processes
- Component information on the availability, reliability and maintainability requirements for the technology components that underpin IT service(s)
- Past performance, unavailability and failure information.

Key outputs from the availability management process include:

■ The availability plan
■ Availability and recovery design criteria and proposed service targets for new or changed services
■ Service and component availability, reliability and maintainability reports of achievements against targets, including input for all service reports
■ Revised risk assessment reviews and the planned and preventive maintenance schedules.

Key interfaces with the availability management process include:

■ **SLM**   Relies on availability management to determine and validate availability targets and to investigate and resolve service and component breaches.
■ **Capacity management**   Provides appropriate capacity to support resilience and service availability.
■ **IT service continuity management (ITSCM)**   This process operates in collaboration with availability management to assess business impact and risk, and provide resilience, fail-over and recovery mechanisms.
■ **Information security management (ISM)**   Defines the security measures and policies that must be included in the service design for availability and recovery.

4.4.7   Critical success factors and key performance indicators

Examples of CSFs and KPIs for the availability management process include:

■ **CSF**   Manage availability and reliability of IT services
  – **KPI**   Percentage reduction in the unavailability of services and components
  – **KPI**   Percentage improvement in overall end-to-end availability of services

- **KPI**   Percentage reduction in the number and impact of service breaks
- **CSF**   Satisfy business needs for access to IT services
  - **KPI**   Percentage reduction in the unavailability of services
  - **KPI**   Percentage reduction of the cost of business overtime due to unavailable IT
  - **KPI**   Percentage reduction in critical time failures – for example, specific business peak and priority availability needs are planned for.

4.4.8   Challenges and risks

Key challenges to the availability management process include:

- Meeting and managing the expectations of the business, customers and senior management
- Integrating data from many sources into information that can be analysed in a consistent and meaningful manner
- Convincing the business and senior management to invest in proactive availability measures.

Some of the major risks associated with availability management include:

- Lack of commitment from the business and lack of information on future plans and strategies
- Lack of senior management commitment or lack of resources and/or budget
- Labour-intensive reporting processes
- The processes focus too much on the technology and not enough on the services and the needs of the business.

4.5   CAPACITY MANAGEMENT

4.5.1   Purpose and objectives

The purpose of the capacity management process is to ensure that the capacity of IT services and the IT infrastructure meets the agreed capacity- and performance-related requirements in a cost-effective and timely manner. Capacity management is concerned with meeting both the current and future capacity and performance needs of the business.

The objectives of capacity management are to:

- Produce and maintain an up-to-date capacity plan
- Provide advice and guidance on all capacity- and performance-related issues
- Ensure that service performance meets all agreed targets by managing the performance and capacity of both services and resources
- Assist with the diagnosis and resolution of performance- and capacity-related incidents and problems
- Ensure that proactive measures to improve the performance of services are implemented.

4.5.2   Scope

The capacity management process should be the focal point for all IT performance and capacity issues. Capacity management considers all resources required to deliver the IT service, and plans for short-, medium- and long-term business requirements.

4.5.3   Value to business

A well-executed capacity management process will benefit the business by:

- Improving the performance, availability and cost effectiveness of IT services that the business needs
- Contributing to customer satisfaction and user productivity by ensuring that all capacity- and performance-related service levels are met
- Supporting the efficient and effective design and transition of new or changed services.

4.5.4   Policies, principles and basic concepts

Capacity management is about balancing opposing factors:

- Balancing costs against required resources
- Balancing supply against demand.

Policies should be defined which specify the necessary interfaces between capacity management and SLM to ensure that this connection to business requirements is established and maintained. Capacity management needs to understand the total IT and business environments.

Capacity management is an extremely technical, complex and demanding process; in order to achieve results it requires three supporting sub-processes:

- **Business capacity management**   Translates business needs and plans into requirements for service and IT infrastructure, ensuring that the future business requirements for IT services are quantified, designed, planned and implemented in a timely fashion.
- **Service capacity management**   Focuses on the management, control and prediction of the end-to-end performance and capacity of live IT services usage and workloads.
- **Component capacity management**   Focuses on the management, control and prediction of the performance, utilization and capacity of individual technology components.

4.5.5 Process activities, methods and techniques

Some activities in the capacity management process are reactive, while others are proactive.

4.5.5.1 The key proactive activities of capacity management

- Pre-empting performance issues
- Modelling and trending predicted changes in IT services (including service retirements), and identifying changes to services and components of the IT infrastructure and applications needed to ensure that appropriate resource is available
- Ensuring that upgrades are budgeted, planned and implemented before SLAs and service targets are breached or performance issues occur
- Actively seeking to improve service performance wherever it is cost-justifiable
- Tuning (optimizing) the performance of services and components.

4.5.5.2 The key reactive activities of capacity management

- Monitoring, measuring, reporting and reviewing the performance of services and components
- Responding to capacity-related 'threshold' events and instigating corrective action
- Reacting to and assisting with performance issues.

Figure 4.3 provides a high-level overview of the capacity management process with its sub-processes, related documents and data, as well as the relationships to capacity management tools.

There are ongoing iterative activities that support capacity management, and these activities can be done both reactively and proactively. The major differences in these activities

Figure 4.3 Capacity management overview with sub-processes

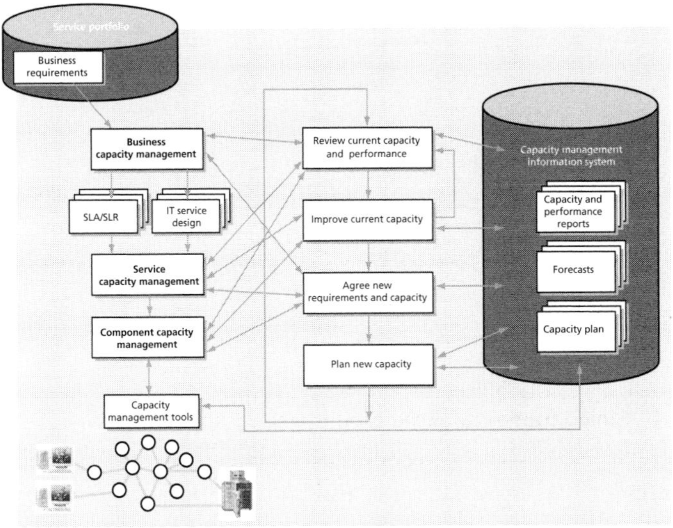

between the sub-processes are in the data that is monitored and collected, and the perspective from which the data is analysed. Many iterative activities form a natural cycle, as illustrated in Figure 4.4. The primary cycle consists of:

- **Monitoring**   To collect the relevant data
- **Analysis**   To determine what the data means
- **Tuning**   To determine the appropriate actions to undertake, based on the results of the analysis
- **Implementation**   To introduce the recommended actions into the live operational environment.

Figure 4.4 Ongoing iterative activities of capacity management

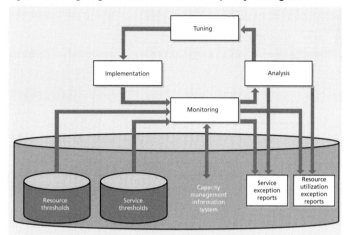

4.5.6   Triggers, inputs, outputs and interfaces

Key triggers for the capacity management process include:

■ New and changed services requiring additional capacity
■ Service breaches, capacity or performance events and alerts
■ Periodic trending and modelling, and periodic review of capacity and performance, forecasts, reports and plans
■ Review and revision of designs and strategies
■ Review and revision of SLRs, SLAs, OLAs, contracts or any other agreements.

Key inputs to the capacity management process include:

- Business, service and IT information, including strategies, plans, budgets, and relationships to technology, infrastructures, environment, data and applications
- Component performance and capacity information
- Service performance issue information
- Service information, with details of the services from the service portfolio, the service catalogue and service level targets within SLAs and SLRs.

Key outputs from the capacity management process include:

- Data, reports and plans, including the capacity plan, service performance information, workload analysis, ad hoc capacity and performance reports, forecasts and predictive reports
- Thresholds, alerts and events
- Improvement actions.

Key interfaces with the capacity management process include:

- **Availability management**   Works with capacity management to determine the resources needed to ensure the required availability of services and components.
- **Service level management**   Capacity management helps to determine capacity targets and investigate service and component capacity-related breaches.
- **ITSCM**   Capacity management assists with the assessment of business impact and risk and determining the capacity needed for risk management.
- **Demand management**   Provides strategic decision-making and critical related data on which capacity management can act.

4.5.7   Critical success factors and key performance indicators

A key example of a CSF and KPIs for the capacity management process is:

- **CSF**   Ability to plan and implement the appropriate IT capacity to match business need
    - **KPI**   Percentage reduction in the number of incidents due to poor performance
    - **KPI**   All new services implemented match SLRs
    - **KPI**   Reduction in the number of SLA breaches due to either poor service performance or poor component performance.

4.5.8   Challenges and risks

Key challenges to capacity management include:

- Obtaining strategic business plans for effective business capacity management
- Combining the component capacity management data into an integrated set of information that can be analysed in a consistent manner.

Key risks to capacity management include:

- A lack of appropriate information from the business on future plans and strategies
- A lack of business and/or senior management commitment or a lack of resources and/or budget
- Service capacity management and component capacity management performed in isolation
- The processes focus too much on the technology and not enough on the services and the business
- The reports and information provided do not give the information that is required or appropriate to the customers and the business.

4.6   IT SERVICE CONTINUITY MANAGEMENT

4.6.1   Purpose and objectives

The purpose of the IT service continuity management process is to support the overall business continuity management (BCM) process by ensuring that, by managing the risks that could seriously affect IT services, the IT service provider can always provide minimum agreed business continuity-related service levels.

In support of and alignment with the BCM process, ITSCM uses formal risk assessment and management techniques to:

- Reduce risks to IT services to agreed acceptable levels
- Plan and prepare for the recovery of IT services.

BCM is the business process responsible for managing risks that could seriously affect the business. The process involves reducing risks to an acceptable level and planning for the recovery of business processes should a disruption to the business occur.

The key objectives of ITSCM are to:

- Produce and maintain IT service continuity plans and associated mechanisms that support business continuity plans and meet or exceed the agreed business continuity targets
- Complete regular business impact analysis (BIA) exercises to ensure that all continuity plans are maintained in line with changing business impacts and requirements
- Conduct regular risk assessment and management exercises to manage IT services within an agreed level of business risk in conjunction with the business and the availability management and information security management processes
- Assess the impact of all changes on IT service continuity plans and supporting methods and procedures.

4.6.2   Scope

ITSCM focuses on events that the business considers significant enough to be treated as a 'disaster'. ITSCM primarily considers the IT assets and configurations that support the business processes.

4.6.3   Value to business

ITSCM provides an invaluable role in supporting the BCM process. In many organizations, ITSCM is used to raise awareness of continuity requirements, and often to justify and implement a BCM process and business continuity plans.

4.6.4   Policies, principles and basic concepts

ITSCM is a cyclic process through the lifecycle employed to ensure that once service continuity plans have been developed they are kept aligned with business continuity plans and business priorities. Figure 4.5 also shows the role played by BCM within the ITSCM process.

4.6.5   Process activities, methods and techniques

The following sections contain details of each of the stages within the ITSCM lifecycle.

4.6.5.1   Stage 1 – Initiation

The initiation process covers the whole of the organization and consists of the following activities:

■ **Policy setting**   Defines management intention and objectives and should be established and communicated as soon as possible.

■ **Define scope and specify terms of reference**   Includes defining the scope and responsibilities of all staff in the organization.

Figure 4.5 Lifecycle of IT service continuity management

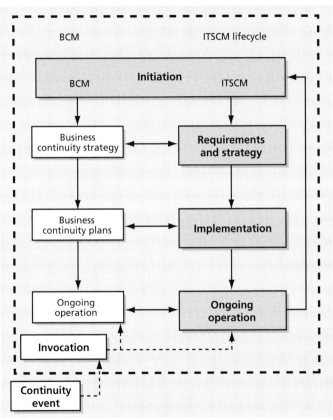

■ **Initiate a project**   The initiation of formal IT service continuity management is best organized into a project.

4.6.5.2   Stage 2 – Requirements and strategy

If the analysis of business requirements for IT service continuity is incorrect, or if key information has been missed, this could have serious consequences for the effectiveness of ITSCM mechanisms. This stage can effectively be split into two sections.

Requirements

Perform BIA and risk assessment. The purpose of a BIA is to quantify the impact to the business that loss of service would have. The BIA will identify the most important services to the organization and will be a key input to the strategy.

The second driver in determining ITSCM requirements is the likelihood that a serious service disruption will actually occur. This is an assessment of the level of threat and the extent to which an organization is vulnerable to that threat.

Strategy

Following the requirements analysis, the strategy should document how the risks will be managed through risk reduction measures and recovery options.

■ **Risk response measures**   The risk reduction measures need to be implemented in conjunction with availability management, as many of these reduce the probability of failure affecting the availability of service.
■ **ITSCM recovery options**   An organization's ITSCM strategy is a balance between the cost of risk reduction measures and recovery options to support the recovery of critical business processes within agreed timescales.

4.6.5.3 Stage 3 – Implementation

Once the strategy has been approved, detailed IT service continuity plans should be produced in line with the business continuity plans, and the measures to implement the strategy need to be put in place. Measures to implement the strategy will include implementing both the defined risk reduction and recovery option arrangements, and performing initial testing to ensure that what was planned has been achieved.

Activities that should follow the approval of the strategy are:

- Organization planning
- Risk reduction/recovery arrangement implementation
- Initial testing.

4.6.5.4 Stage 4 – Ongoing operation

This stage consists of activities to establish and maintain ITSCM capabilities. Maintaining the relevance of ITSCM requires regular BIA and risk assessment and management activities in cooperation with BCM, and action to implement changes based on any resulting strategy revisions. The activities of ongoing operation include:

- Education, awareness and training
- Review and audit
- Testing
- Change management.

4.6.5.5 Invocation

Invocation is a key component of the plans, which must include the invocation process and guidance. This decision is typically made by a 'crisis management' team, comprising senior managers from the business and support departments (including

IT), using information gathered through damage assessment and other sources.

4.6.6   Triggers, inputs, outputs and interfaces

Key triggers for the IT service continuity management process include:

- New or changed business needs, services or targets within agreements, such as SLRs, SLAs, OLAs or contracts
- Periodic activities such as BIA or risk assessment, maintenance of continuity plans or other reviewing, revising or reporting activities
- Review and revision of changes, designs and strategies
- Initiation of tests of continuity and recovery plans.

Key inputs to the IT service continuity management process include:

- Business information from the organization's business strategy, plans and financial plans, and information on their current and future requirements
- A business continuity strategy and business continuity plans from all areas of the business
- Service information with details of the services from the service portfolio and the service catalogue, and service level targets within SLAs and SLRs.

Key outputs from the IT service continuity management process include:

- ITSCM policy and strategy
- Detailed and integrated ITSCM plans
- BIA exercises and reports, in conjunction with BCM and the business

- Risk assessment and management reviews and reports, in conjunction with the business, availability management and information security management
- An ITSCM testing schedule, test scenarios, test reports and reviews.

Key interfaces with the IT service continuity management process include:

- **Change management**   All changes need to be considered for their impact on continuity plans. Continuity plans must be under change management control.
- **Availability management**   Undertaking risk assessment and implementing risk responses should be coordinated with availability management.
- **Service level management**   Recovery requirements and service levels during a continuity event will be agreed and documented in SLAs.
- **Information security management**   A major security breach could be considered a disaster, so when conducting BIA and risk assessment, security will be an important consideration.

4.6.7   Critical success factors and key performance indicators

A key example of a CSF and KPIs for the IT service continuity management process is:

- **CSF**   IT services are delivered and can be recovered to meet business objectives
  - **KPI**   Increase in success of regular audits of the ITSCM plans to ensure that, at all times, the agreed recovery requirements of the business can be achieved
  - **KPI**   Regular successful validation to check that all service recovery targets are agreed and documented in SLAs and are achievable within the ITSCM plans
  - **KPI**   Regular and comprehensive testing of ITSCM plans.

4.6.8   Challenges and risks

Key challenges for the IT service continuity process include:

- Providing appropriate plans when there is no BCM process
- Proper alignment between ITSCM plans and the BCM plan.

Key risks to the IT service continuity process include:

- Lack of a BCM process or appropriate information on business plans and strategies
- Lack of business and/or senior management commitment, or lack of resources and/or budget
- Risk assessment and management are conducted in isolation and not in conjunction with availability management and information security management
- ITSCM plans and information become out of date and lose alignment with the information and plans of the business and BCM.

4.7   INFORMATION SECURITY MANAGEMENT

4.7.1   Purpose and objectives

The purpose of the information security management (ISM) process is to align IT security with business security and ensure that the confidentiality, integrity and availability of the organization's assets, information, data and IT services always match the agreed needs of the business.

The objective of ISM is to protect the interests of those relying on information, and the systems and communications that deliver the information, from harm resulting from failures of confidentiality, integrity and availability.

For most organizations, the security objective is met when:

- Information is observed by or disclosed only to those who have a right to know (confidentiality)
- Information is complete, accurate and protected against unauthorized modification (integrity)
- Information is available and usable when required, and the systems that provide it can appropriately resist attacks and recover from or prevent failures (availability)
- Business transactions, as well as information exchanges between enterprises, or with partners, can be trusted (authenticity and non-repudiation).

4.7.2   Scope

The ISM process should be the focal point for all IT security issues, and must ensure that an information security policy is produced, maintained and enforced that covers the use and misuse of all IT systems and services. Information security management needs to understand the total IT and business security environment to ensure that all the current and future security aspects and risks of the business are managed cost-effectively.

4.7.3   Value to business

Information security management provides assurance of business processes by enforcing appropriate security controls in all areas of IT and by managing IT risk in line with business and corporate risk management processes and guidelines.

4.7.4   Policies, principles and basic concepts

Information security management activities should be focused on and driven by an overall information security policy and a set of underpinning specific security policies. The information security policy should have the full support of top executive

Figure 4.6 Elements of an ISMS for managing IT security

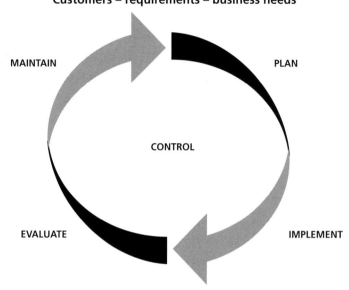

IT management and ideally the support and commitment of top executive business management. The policy should be appropriate, meet the needs of the business and cover all areas of security. In most cases, these policies should be widely available to all customers and users, and their compliance should be referred to in all SLRs, SLAs, OLAs, underpinning contracts and agreements.

The ISM process will have a formal system to establish policy and objectives and to achieve those objectives. ISO/IEC 27001 is the formal standard against which organizations may seek independent certification of their information security management system (ISMS). The ISMS illustrated in Figure 4.6 shows an approach that is widely used and is based on the advice and guidance described in many sources, including ISO/IEC 27001.

The five elements within this structure are:

- **Control**   To establish a management framework to initiate and manage information security in the organization, implement the information security policy and control roles and documentation
- **Plan**   To devise and recommend appropriate security measures, based on understanding the requirements of the organization
- **Implement**   To ensure that appropriate procedures, tools and controls are in place to underpin the information security policy
- **Evaluate**   To supervise and check compliance with the security policy by carrying out regular audits, and providing information to external auditors, when required
- **Maintain**   To improve security agreements as specified in, for example, SLAs and OLAs and improve security measures and controls.

4.7.5 Process activities, methods and techniques

The key activities within the ISM process are as follows.

4.7.5.1 Security policy management

This activity includes production, maintenance and enforcement of an overall information security policy and a set of supporting specific policies.

Figure 4.7 Security controls for threats and incidents

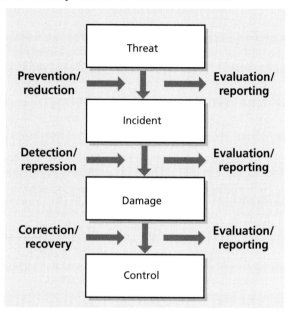

4.7.5.2   Security controls

This activity includes implementation, review, revision and improvement of security controls as well as risk assessment and responses. Information security must be an integral part of all services and systems, and is an ongoing process that needs to be continuously managed using a set of security controls.

The security controls should be designed to support and enforce the information security policy and to minimize threats. Security measures can be used at a specific stage in the prevention and handling of security incidents, as illustrated in Figure 4.7. These measures include:

- **Preventive**   Security measures used to prevent a security incident from occurring
- **Reductive**   Further measures taken in advance to minimize any possible damage that may occur
- **Detective**   If a security incident occurs, it is important to discover it as soon as possible
- **Repressive**   Measures are then used to counteract any continuation or repetition of the incident
- **Corrective**   The damage is repaired as far as possible using corrective measures.

4.7.5.3 Security incident management

This activity includes monitoring, management, analysis and reduction of all security breaches and major security incidents. In the case of serious security breaches or incidents, an evaluation is necessary to determine what went wrong, what caused it and how it can be prevented in the future. However, this process should not be limited to serious security incidents. All breaches of security and security incidents need to be studied to gain a full picture of the effectiveness of the security measures as a whole.

4.7.5.4 Security auditing and testing

This activity includes scheduling and completion of security reviews, audits and penetration tests.

4.7.6 Triggers, inputs, outputs and interfaces

Key triggers for the ISM process include:

- New or changed business needs, services, corporate governance guidelines, business security policies, or corporate risk management processes and guidelines
- New or changed requirements within agreements, such as SLRs, SLAs, OLAs or contracts
- Service or component security breaches or warnings, events and alerts, including threshold events, exception reports
- Periodic activities, such as reviewing, revising or reporting, including review and revision of ISM policies, reports and plans
- Change of risk or impact to a business process or VBF, an IT service or component.

Key inputs to the ISM process include:

- **Business information**   Including business strategy, plans (including financial plans), current and future requirements, corporate governance information, business security policies and guidelines, security plans, risk assessment and responses
- **IT information**   The IT strategy and plans and current budgets
- **Service information**   Including details of services from the service portfolio and service catalogue, and service level targets within SLAs and SLRs
- **Information**   From other service management processes.

Key outputs from the ISM process include:

- An overall ISM policy and specific security policies
- Revised security risk assessment processes and reports
- Security controls, together with details of their operation and maintenance and their associated risks

- Security audits and audit reports, test schedules, plans and test reports.

Key interfaces with the ISM process include:

- **Service level management**   ISM provides assistance with determining security requirements and responsibilities and their inclusion within SLRs and SLAs.
- **Access management**   This process grants and revokes access and applies the policies defined by ISM.
- **IT service continuity management**   ISM works collaboratively with ITSCM on the assessment of business impact and risk, and the provision of resilience, fail-over and recovery mechanisms.
- **Availability management**   ISM is a critical enabler of availability management. Availability management is responsible for ensuring that security requirements are defined and incorporated within the availability design.

4.7.7   Critical success factors and key performance indicators

Examples of CSFs and KPIs for the ISM process include:

- **CSF**   Business is protected against security violations
  - **KPI**   Percentage decrease in security breaches
  - **KPI**   Percentage decrease in the impact of security breaches and incidents
- **CSF**   The availability of services is not compromised by security incidents
  - **KPI**   Percentage decrease in the impact of security breaches and incidents
  - **KPI**   Percentage reduction in the number of incidents of service unavailability linked to security breaches.

4.7.8   Challenges and risks

Key challenges for the ISM process include:

- Ensuring that there is adequate support from the business, business security and senior management
- Maintaining proper integration and alignment with corporate security.

Key risks to the ISM process include:

- External dangers from hackers, leading to denial of service and virus attacks, extortion, industrial espionage and leakage of organizational information or private data.
- A lack of business and/or senior management commitment or a lack of resources and/or budget.
- The processes focus too much on technology and not enough on IT services and the needs and priorities of the business.
- Information security management policies, plans, risks and information become out of date.
- Security policies become bureaucratic and/or excessively difficult to follow, discouraging compliance or adding no value to business.

4.8   SUPPLIER MANAGEMENT

4.8.1   Purpose and objectives

The purpose of the supplier management process is to obtain value for money from suppliers and to provide seamless quality of IT service to the business by ensuring that all contracts and agreements with suppliers support the needs of the business and that all suppliers meet their contractual commitments.

The key objectives of the supplier management process are to:

- Obtain value for money from suppliers and contracts

- Ensure that contracts with suppliers are aligned to business needs, and support and align with agreed targets in SLRs and SLAs, in conjunction with SLM
- Manage relationships with suppliers and supplier performance
- Negotiate and agree contracts with suppliers and manage them through their lifecycle.

4.8.2 Scope

The supplier management process should include the management of all suppliers and contracts needed to support the provision of IT services to the business. Each service provider should have formal processes for the management of all suppliers and contracts.

4.8.3 Value to business

Supplier management ensures that the business obtains value from supporting supplier services and that they are aligned with business needs.

4.8.4 Policies, principles and basic concepts

All supplier management activity should be driven by a supplier strategy and policy. Supplier policies adopted by an organization may cover such areas as:

- The acceptable methods for communication with potential suppliers before and during solicitation, bidding and procurement
- Who is authorized to interact with suppliers
- Supplier standards – for example, all suppliers for a hospital in the US must be compliant with the Health Insurance Portability and Accountability Act

■ Standards and guidelines for various supplier contract types and/or agreement types.

4.8.4.1 Underpinning contracts and agreements

The nature and extent of an agreement between a service provider and supplier depends on the relationship type and an assessment of the risks involved. A comprehensive agreement minimizes the risk of disputes arising from a difference of expectations. A flexible agreement, which adequately caters for its adaptation across the term of the agreement, is maintainable and supports change with a minimum amount of renegotiation.

4.8.5 Process activities, methods and techniques

When dealing with external suppliers, it is strongly recommended that a formal contract with clearly defined, agreed and documented responsibilities and targets is established and managed through the stages of its lifecycle, from identification of the business need to operation and cessation of the contract.

The key activities of supplier management can be summarized as follows.

4.8.5.1 Requirements development

This involves definition of new supplier and contract requirements, including preparation of the business case with options (internal and external), costs, timescales, targets, benefits and risk assessment.

4.8.5.2 Evaluation and establishment of new suppliers and contracts

This activity includes establishing evaluation criteria, evaluating alternative options, selecting the supplier, and negotiating contracts. Contract negotiation and establishment should ensure that supplier targets are aligned with commitments in SLRs and SLAs.

4.8.5.3 Supplier, contract and performance management

This activity includes managing, controlling, monitoring, reporting, reviewing and improving the operation and delivery of service/products, management of the supplier and the relationship, and planning for possible closure/renewal/extension.

4.8.5.4 Contract renewal or termination

The tasks for this activity are to review the previous contract, renegotiate and renew or terminate and/or transfer, and if necessary, transition to new supplier(s) or to internal resources.

The business, IT, finance, purchasing and procurement need to work together to ensure that all stages of the contract lifecycle are managed effectively. The activities involved in the stages of the contract lifecycle are illustrated in Figure 4.8, along with a representation of the supplier and contract management information system (SCMIS).

4.8.5.5 Supplier categorization

The supplier management process should be adaptive; more time and effort should be spent on managing key suppliers than is devoted to the less important ones. This means that some form of categorization scheme is needed to classify suppliers and evaluate their importance to the service provider and the services provided to the business. Suppliers can be categorized in many ways, but one of the best methods is based on assessing the risk and impact associated with using the supplier, and the

Figure 4.8 Supplier management process

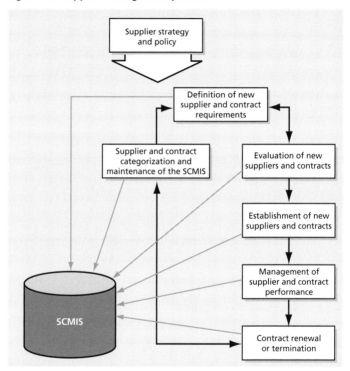

value and importance of the supplier and its services to the business, as illustrated in Figure 4.9.

The amount of time and effort spent managing the supplier and the relationship can then be appropriate to its categorization:

Figure 4.9 Supplier categorization

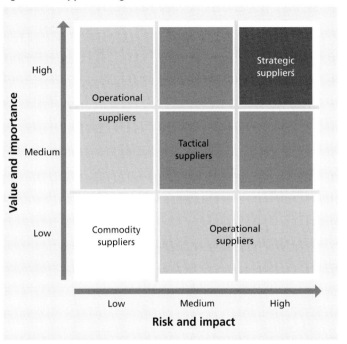

- ■ **Strategic**   Significant 'partnering' relationships that involve senior managers sharing confidential strategic information to facilitate long-term plans
- ■ **Tactical**   Relationships involving significant commercial activity and business interaction
- ■ **Operational**   Suppliers of operational products or services

■ **Commodity**   Suppliers providing low-value and/or readily available products and services, which could be alternatively sourced relatively easily.

4.8.6   Triggers, inputs, outputs and interfaces

Key triggers for the supplier management process include:

■ New or changed business needs, services, corporate governance guidelines, business and IT strategies, policies or plans
■ New or changed requirements within agreements, such as SLRs, SLAs, OLAs or contracts
■ Requests from other areas, particularly SLM and ISM, for assistance with supplier issues
■ Requirements for new contracts, contract renewal or contract termination.

Key inputs to the supplier management process include:

■ Business information, including business strategy, plans, financial information, and information on current and future business requirements
■ Supplier and contracts strategy
■ Supplier contracts, agreements and targets and performance information of both existing and new contracts and agreements from suppliers
■ IT information, including IT strategy, plans and budgets
■ Service information with details of the services from the service portfolio and the service catalogue, service level targets within SLAs and SLRs, and possibly from the monitoring of SLAs, service reviews and breaches of the SLAs.

Key outputs from the supplier management process include:

■ Supplier and contract performance information and reports
■ Supplier SIPs.

Key interfaces with the supplier management process include:

- **SLM**   Supplier management provides assistance with determining targets, requirements and responsibilities for suppliers. It sees to their inclusion within underpinning agreements and contracts to ensure that they support all SLR and SLA targets.
- **ISM**   ISM relies on supplier management for the management of suppliers and their access to services and systems, and their responsibilities with regard to conformance to the service provider's ISM policies and requirements.
- **Service portfolio management**   This process looks to supplier management input to ensure that all supporting services and their details and relationships are accurately reflected within the service portfolio.
- **ITSCM**   This process works with supplier management with regard to the management of continuity service suppliers.

4.8.7   Critical success factors and key performance indicators

Examples of CSFs and KPIs for the supplier management process include:

- **CSF**   Business protected from poor supplier performance or disruption
    - **KPI**   Increase in the number of suppliers meeting the targets within the contract
    - **KPI**   Reduction in the number of breaches of contractual targets
- **CSF**   Supporting services and their targets align with business needs and targets
    - **KPI**   Increase in the number of service and contractual reviews held with suppliers

- **KPI** Increase in the number of supplier and contractual targets aligned with SLA and SLR targets

4.8.8 Challenges and risks

Key challenges for the supplier management process include:

- Working with an imposed non-ideal contract
- Being tied into long-term contracts, with no possibility of improvement, which have punitive penalty charges for early exit
- Poor communication – not interacting often enough or quickly enough, or not focusing on the right issues.

Key risks to the supplier management process include:

- Legacy of badly written and agreed contracts that do not underpin or support business needs or SLA and SLR targets
- Suppliers agreeing to targets and service levels within contracts that are impossible to meet, or suppliers failing or being incapable of meeting the terms and conditions of the contract
- Lack of clarity and insufficient integration by a supplier with the service management processes, policies and procedures of the service provider
- Poor corporate financial processes, such as procurement and purchasing, which do not support good supplier management.

5 Organizing for service design

There is no single best way to organize, and best practices described in ITIL need to be tailored to suit each situation, taking into account resource constraints and the size, nature and needs of the business and customers. The starting point for organizational design is service strategy.

Section 2.2.3 of this publication provides an overview of functions and roles.

5.1 FUNCTIONS

For service design to be successful, an organization will need to define the roles and responsibilities required to undertake the processes and activities identified in this key element guide. These roles should be assigned to individuals, and an appropriate organization structure of teams, groups or functions established and managed.

Service design does not define specific functions, but it does rely on the technical and application management functions described in *ITIL Service Operation*. Technical and application management provide resources and expertise to manage the whole service lifecycle, and roles within service design may be performed by members of these functions.

5.1.1 Alignment with application development

If an application development function exists inside the service provider, it will focus on building functionality – that is, the utility – required by the business. Historically, what the application does is more important to this team than how the application is operated. This is why the input of application management, technical management, IT operations management and the service desk should be sought during service design to ensure that the output of service design will meet all customer needs, not just those related to functionality.

Most application development work is performed as part of projects where the focus is on delivering specific units of work to specification, on time and within budget.

The application development function utilizes software development lifecycles to provide formal structure to its work. This work must be integrated into the overall service lifecycle, as the applications to be developed form a central part of the IT services provisioned by the IT service provider.

5.1.2 Alignment with project management

Another function that may exist is project management, sometimes called the project management office (PMO). The purpose of this team is to define and maintain the service provider's project management standards and to provide resources and management of IT projects.

If a project management function exists, it will be actively involved in the work of the service design and service transition stages of the service lifecycle, as well as during any other temporary endeavour that would benefit from application of formal project management.

Project portfolio management interfaces with service portfolio management, ensures that resources are appropriately allocated across the complete set of projects being managed and maximizes project success.

5.2   ROLES

A number of roles need to be performed in support of service design. The core ITIL publications provide guidelines and examples of role descriptions. In many cases roles will need to be combined or separated depending on the organizational context and size.

A RACI model can be used to define the roles and responsibilities in relation to processes and activities.

RACI is an acronym for:

- **Responsible**   The person or people responsible for correct execution – for getting the job done.
- **Accountable**   The person who has ownership of quality and the end result.
- **Consulted**   The people who are consulted and whose opinions are sought. They have involvement through input of knowledge and information.
- **Informed**   The people who are kept up to date on progress. They receive information about process execution and quality.

Only one person should be accountable for any process or individual activity, although several people may be responsible for executing parts of the activity.

Roles fall into two main categories – generic roles such as process manager and process owner, and specific roles that are involved within a particular lifecycle stage or process, such as a change administrator or knowledge management process owner.

5.2.1 Generic service owner role

The service owner is accountable for the delivery of a specific IT service and is responsible for the initiation, transition, maintenance and support of that service.

The service owner's responsibilities include:

- Working with business relationship management to ensure that the service provider can meet customer requirements
- Participating in negotiating service level agreements (SLAs) and operational level agreements (OLAs) relating to the service
- Ensuring that ongoing service delivery and support meet agreed customer requirements
- Ensuring consistent and appropriate communication with customer(s) for service-related enquiries and issues
- Representing the service across the organization, including at change advisory board (CAB) meetings
- Serving as the point of escalation (notification) for major incidents relating to the service
- Participating in internal and external service review meetings.

The service owner is responsible for continual improvement and the management of change affecting the service under their care.

5.2.2 Generic process owner role

The process owner role is accountable for ensuring that a process is fit for purpose, is performed according to agreed standards and meets the aims of the process definition. This role is often assigned to the same person who carries out the process manager role, but the two roles may be separate in larger organizations.

The process owner's accountabilities include:

- Sponsoring, designing and change managing the process and its metrics
- Defining appropriate policies and standards for the process, with periodic auditing to ensure compliance
- Providing process resources to support activities required throughout the service lifecycle
- Ensuring that process technicians understand their role and have the required knowledge to deliver the process
- Addressing issues with running the process
- Identifying enhancement and improvement opportunities and making improvements to the process.

5.2.3   Generic process manager role

The process manager role is accountable for operational management of a process. There may be several process managers for one process, for example covering different locations.

The process manager's accountabilities include:

- Working with the process owner to plan and coordinate all process activities
- Ensuring that all activities are carried out as required throughout the service lifecycle
- Appointing people to the required roles and managing assigned resources
- Monitoring and reporting on process performance
- Identifying opportunities for and making improvements to the process.

5.2.4   Generic process practitioner role

The process practitioner's responsibilities include:

- Carrying out one or more activities of a process

- Understanding how their role contributes to the overall delivery of service and creation of value for the business
- Ensuring that inputs, outputs and interfaces for their activities are correct
- Creating or updating records to show that activities have been carried out correctly.

5.2.5   Design coordination roles

5.2.5.1   Design coordination process owner

The design coordination process owner's responsibilities typically include:

- Carrying out the generic process owner role for design coordination
- Setting the scope and policies for service design
- Overseeing the design of all service design processes to ensure that they will work together to meet the needs of the business.

5.2.5.2   Design coordination process manager

The design coordination process manager's key responsibilities are focused around the operational management of the objectives and activities of design coordination, as described in section 4.1 of this key element guide.

5.2.6   Service catalogue management roles

5.2.6.1   Service catalogue management process owner

The service catalogue management process owner's responsibilities typically include:

- Carrying out the generic process owner role for service catalogue management

■ Working with other process owners to ensure that there is an integrated approach to the design and implementation of service catalogue management, service portfolio management, service level management and business relationship management.

5.2.6.2 Service catalogue management process manager

The service catalogue management process manager's responsibilities are focused around the operational management of the objectives and activities of service catalogue management, as described in section 4.2 of this key element guide.

5.2.7 Service level management roles

5.2.7.1 Service level management process owner

The service level management process owner's responsibilities typically include:

■ Carrying out the generic process owner role for service level management
■ Liaising with the business relationship management process owner to ensure proper coordination and communication between the two processes
■ Working with other process owners to ensure that there is an integrated approach to the design and implementation of service catalogue management, service portfolio management, service level management and business relationship management.

5.2.7.2 Service level management process manager

The service level management process manager's responsibilities are focused around the operational management of the objectives and activities of service level management, as described in section 4.3 of this key element guide.

These next two roles, while not strictly speaking service level management roles, typically play a large part in the successful execution of the process.

5.2.7.3   Service owner role in service level management

Persons assigned to the role of service owner participate in the service level management process by:

- Ensuring that service delivery and support meet agreed customer requirements
- Ensuring consistent and appropriate communication with customer(s) for service-related enquiries and issues
- Providing input on service attributes such as performance and availability
- Participating in service review meetings with the business
- Soliciting required data, statistics and reports for analysis and to facilitate effective service monitoring and performance
- Participating in negotiating SLAs and OLAs relating to the service.

5.2.7.4   Business relationship manager role in service level management

Persons assigned to the role of business relationship manager participate in the service level management process by:

- Ensuring high levels of customer satisfaction
- Establishing and maintaining a constructive relationship between the service provider and the customer at a strategic level
- Confirming customer high-level requirements

- Facilitating service level agreement negotiations by ensuring that the correct customer representatives participate
- Identifying opportunities for improvement.

5.2.8 Availability management roles

5.2.8.1 Availability management process owner

The availability management process owner's responsibilities typically include:

- Carrying out the generic process owner role for availability management
- Working with managers of all functions to ensure acceptance of the availability management process as the single point of coordination for availability-related issues, regardless of the specific technology involved
- Working with other process owners to ensure that there is an integrated approach to the design and implementation of availability management, service level management, capacity management, IT service continuity management and information security management.

5.2.8.2 Availability management process manager

The availability management process manager's key responsibilities are focused around the operational management of the objectives and activities of availability management, as described in section 4.4 of this key element guide.

5.2.9 Capacity management roles

5.2.9.1 Capacity management process owner

The capacity management process owner's responsibilities typically include:

- Carrying out the generic process owner role for capacity management
- Working with managers of all functions to ensure acceptance of the capacity management process as the single point of coordination for all capacity and performance-related issues, regardless of the specific technology involved
- Working with other process owners to ensure that there is an integrated approach to the design and implementation of capacity management, availability management, IT service continuity management and information security management.

5.2.9.2   Capacity management process manager

The capacity management process manager's responsibilities are focused around the operational management of the objectives and activities of capacity management, as described in section 4.5 of this key element guide.

5.2.10   IT service continuity management roles

5.2.10.1   IT service continuity management process owner

The IT service continuity management process owner's responsibilities typically include:

- Carrying out the generic process owner role for ITSCM
- Working with the business to ensure proper coordination and communication between business continuity management and ITSCM
- Working with managers of all functions to ensure acceptance of the ITSCM process as the single point of coordination for all IT service continuity-related issues, regardless of the technology involved

- Working with other process owners to ensure that there is an integrated approach to the design and implementation of ITSCM, information security management, availability management and business continuity management.

5.2.10.2 IT service continuity management process manager

The IT service continuity management process manager's responsibilities are focused around the operational management of the objectives and activities of ITSCM, as described in section 4.6 of this key element guide.

5.2.11 Information security management roles

5.2.11.1 Information security management process owner

The information security management process owner's responsibilities typically include:

- Carrying out the generic process owner role for ISM
- Working with the business to ensure proper coordination and communication between organizational (business) security management and ISM
- Working with managers of all functions to ensure acceptance of the ISM process as the single point of coordination for all information security-related issues, regardless of the specific technology involved
- Working with other process owners to ensure there is an integrated approach to the design and implementation of ISM, availability management, IT service continuity management and organizational security management.

5.2.11.2 Information security management process manager

The information security management process manager's responsibilities are focused around the operational management of the objectives and activities of ISM, as described in section 4.7 of this key element guide.

5.2.12 Supplier management roles

5.2.12.1 Supplier management process owner

The supplier management process owner's responsibilities typically include:

- Carrying out the generic process owner role for supplier management
- Working with the business to ensure proper coordination and communication between corporate vendor management and/or procurement and supplier management
- Working with other process owners to ensure that there is an integrated approach to the design and implementation of supplier management, service level management and corporate vendor management and/or procurement processes.

5.2.12.2 Supplier management process manager

The supplier management process manager's responsibilities are focused around the operational management of the objectives and activities of supplier management, as described in section 4.8 of this key element guide.

5.2.13 Other service design roles

A number of roles may exist to support the service design stage of the service lifecycle, two of which are briefly described here. Some of these roles may also include responsibilities associated with other service lifecycle stages. Responsibilities described may also be reorganized into other roles based on the organization's needs and objectives.

- **IT planner**   Responsible for the production and coordination of IT plans
- **IT designer/architect**   Responsible for the overall coordination and design of the required technology.

6 Implementing service design

6.1 RISKS TO THE SERVICES AND PROCESSES

When implementing the service design processes, business-as-usual practices must not be adversely affected. This aspect must be considered during the production and selection of the preferred solution to ensure that disruption to operational services is minimized. This assessment of risk should then be considered in detail in the service transition activities as part of the implementation process.

6.2 IMPLEMENTING SERVICE DESIGN

6.2.1 Where do we start?

The question often asked is 'Which process shall I implement first?' It is recommended that the areas of greatest need be addressed first. A detailed assessment should be undertaken to ascertain the strengths and weaknesses of IT service provision. It may be that 'quick wins' need to be implemented to improve the current situation, but these improved processes may have to be discarded or amended as part of medium- or long-term strategies. Implementation priorities should be set against the goals of a service improvement plan (SIP).

6.2.2 How do we improve?

The first thing to do is to establish a formal process and method of implementation and improvement of service design, with appropriate governance in place. This process should be based around the six-stage approach illustrated in Figure 6.1. It is important that, when implementing or improving processes, a structured project management method is used. The improvement process can be summarized as:

■ First, understanding the vision by ascertaining the high-level business objectives. The 'vision-setting' should set and align business and IT strategies.
■ Second, assessing the current situation to identify strengths that can be built on and weaknesses that need to be addressed. So 'Where are we now?' is an analysis of the current position in terms of the business, organization, people and process.
■ Third, 'Where do we want to be?' is a development of the principles defined in the vision-setting, agreeing the priorities for improvement.

Figure 6.1 Implementation/continual service improvement approach

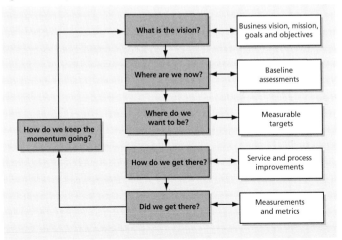

- Fourth, detailing the SIP to achieve higher-quality service provision.
- Next, measurements and metrics need to be put in place to show that the milestones have been achieved and that the business objectives and business priorities have been met.
- Finally, the process should ensure that the momentum for quality improvement is maintained.

6.3   MEASUREMENT OF SERVICE DESIGN

The success of each service design and the success of the process improvement around the service design must be measured, the data must be analysed and reported on. Where the design or process does not meet the requirements of the business as a whole, changes may be required, and the results of those changes must also be measured. Continuous measurement, analysis and reporting are mandatory requirements for both the service design stage and the IT service management processes. There are measurement methods available that enable the analysis of service improvement. More information can be found on measurement methods and techniques in *ITIL Continual Service Improvement*.

7 Challenges, risks and critical success factors

7.1 CHALLENGES

When attempting to design new services and processes that meet the requirements of all stakeholders there will be challenges or difficulties to face and to overcome. Some examples of these challenges are:

- Organizational resistance to change
- Difficulty with adherence to agreed practices and processes
- A lack of understanding of service and business targets, requirements, business impacts and priorities
- Inefficient use of resources, causing wasted time and money
- Poor relationships, communication or lack of cooperation between the IT service provider and the business
- Lack of information, monitoring and measurements
- Unreasonable targets and timescales previously agreed in SLAs and OLAs
- Over-commitment of resources with an inability to deliver (e.g. projects always late or over budget)
- Ensuring that normal daily operation or business as usual is considered as part of the design
- Difficulty in ascertaining the return on investment and the realization of business benefit.

7.2 RISKS

There are a number of risks directly associated with the service design stage of the service lifecycle, including:

- If maturity of one process is low, it will be impossible to achieve full maturity in other processes.
- Business requirements are not clear to IT staff.
- Business timescales give insufficient time for proper service design.
- The fit between infrastructures, customers and partners is not sufficient to meet business requirements.
- The policies and strategies, especially the service management strategy, are not available, or their content is not understood.
- Processes are over- or under-engineered.
- Insufficient resources and budget are available.
- Insufficient time is given to the design stage, or insufficient training is provided for staff tasked with the design.
- There is insufficient engagement with or commitment to the application's functional development, leading to insufficient attention to service design requirements.

7.3 CRITICAL SUCCESS FACTORS

The primary factors for success for the service design stage have to do with service solution designs that meet the documented requirements of the business in a timely and cost-effective manner.

KPIs for the service design stage may include:

- Percentage of service design requirement specifications produced on time and within budget
- Percentage of service design plans produced on time
- Percentage of service design packages completed on time
- Percentage of quality assurance and acceptance criteria plans produced on time

- Accuracy of service design – for example, was the correct infrastructure built to support the service?
- Percentage accuracy of the cost estimate of the whole service design stage
- Accuracy of service level agreement(s), operational level agreement(s) and contract(s) – do they really support the required level of service?

8   Key messages and lessons

Service design, as described in this key element guide, covers the design of appropriate and innovative IT services to meet current and future agreed business requirements. Service design develops an SDP and selects the appropriate service design model. The various sourcing models available and their respective merits have also to be considered.

This publication also discusses the five aspects of service design that must be addressed. It has explained that the better and more careful the design, the better the solution taken into live operation will be. It is also expected that with better design, less re-work time will be needed during the transition and operation stages.

The scope of this key element guide includes the design of services, as well as the design of service management systems and processes. Service design is not limited to new services, but includes change necessary to increase or maintain value to customers over the lifecycle of services.

This publication explains that pragmatism sometimes overrides the perfect solution where the amount of effort and cost does not justify that perfect solution. As always, the solution will depend on the business requirements, and it is imperative that whatever is done with IT has a direct benefit to the overall business.

9 Related guidance

This chapter provides some information about other frameworks, best practices, models and quality systems that have synergy with the ITIL service lifecycle.

9.1 RISK ASSESSMENT AND MANAGEMENT

Risk may be defined as uncertainty of outcome, whether a positive opportunity or negative threat. Formal risk management enables better decision-making based on a sound understanding of risks and their likely impact.

A number of different methodologies, standards and frameworks have been developed for risk management. Each organization should determine the approach to risk management that is best suited to its needs and circumstances.

Approaches to risk management that should be considered include:

- Office of Government Commerce (2010). *Management of Risk: Guidance for Practitioners.* TSO, London.
- ISO 31000
- ISO/IEC 27001
- Risk IT[2]

9.2 ITIL GUIDANCE AND WEB SERVICES

ITIL is part of the Best Management Practice portfolio of best-practice guidance.

The Best Management Practice website (www.best-management-practice.com) includes news, reviews, case studies

[2] With the publication of COBIT 5, Risk IT will be included within COBIT.

and white papers on ITIL and all other Best Management Practice guidance.

The ITIL official website (www.itil-officialsite.com) contains reliable, up-to-date information on ITIL – including information on accreditation and the ITIL software scheme for the endorsement of ITIL-based tools.

Details of the core ITIL publications are:

- Cabinet Office (2011). *ITIL Service Strategy*. TSO, London.
- Cabinet Office (2011). *ITIL Service Design*. TSO, London.
- Cabinet Office (2011). *ITIL Service Transition*. TSO, London.
- Cabinet Office (2011). *ITIL Service Operation*. TSO, London.
- Cabinet Office (2011). *ITIL Continual Service Improvement*. TSO, London.

The full ITIL glossary, in English and other languages, can be accessed through the ITIL official site at:

www.itil-officialsite.com/InternationalActivities/ TranslatedGlossaries.aspx

The full range of ITIL-derived and complementary publications can be found in the publications library of the Best Management Practice website at:

www.best-management-practice.com/Publications-Library/IT-Service-Management-ITIL/

9.3   QUALITY MANAGEMENT SYSTEM

Quality management focuses on product/service quality as well as the quality assurance and control of processes. Total Quality Management (TQM) is a methodology for managing continual improvement by using a quality management system.

ISO 9000:2005 describes the fundamentals of quality management systems that are applicable to all organizations which need to demonstrate their ability to consistently provide products that meet requirements. ISO 9001:2008 specifies generic requirements for a quality management system.

9.4 GOVERNANCE OF IT

ISO 9004 (Managing for the sustained success of an organization – a quality management approach) provides guidance on governance for the board and top management of an organization.

ISO/IEC 38500 is the standard for corporate governance of IT. The purpose of this standard is to promote effective, efficient and acceptable use of IT in all organizations.

9.5 COBIT

The Control OBjectives for Information and related Technology (COBIT) is a governance and control framework for IT management created by ISACA and the IT Governance Institute (ITGI).

COBIT is positioned at a high level, is driven by business requirements, covers the full range of IT activities, and concentrates on *what* should be achieved rather than *how* to achieve effective governance, management and control. ITIL provides an organization with best-practice guidance on *how* to manage and improve its processes to deliver high-quality, cost-effective IT services.

Further information about COBIT is available at www.isaca.org and www.itgi.org

9.6   ISO/IEC 20000 SERVICE MANAGEMENT SERIES

ISO/IEC 20000 is an internationally recognized standard for ITSM covering service providers who manage and deliver IT-enabled services to internal or external customers. ISO/IEC 20000-1 is aligned with other ISO management systems standards such as ISO 9001 and ISO/IEC 27001.

One of the most common routes for an organization to achieve the requirements of ISO/IEC 20000 is by adopting ITIL best practices.

Further details can be found at www.iso.org or www.isoiec20000certification.com

9.7   ENVIRONMENTAL MANAGEMENT AND GREEN/ SUSTAINABLE IT

'Green IT' refers to environmentally sustainable computing where the use and disposal of computers and printers are carried out in sustainable ways that do not have a negative impact on the environment.

The ISO 14001 series of standards for an environment management system is designed to assure internal and external stakeholders that the organization is an environmentally responsible organization.

Further details are available at www.iso.org

9.8   PROGRAMME AND PROJECT MANAGEMENT

The principles of programme management are key to delivering on time and within budget. Best management practice in this area is found in *Managing Successful Programmes* (MSP) (TSO, 2011).

Visit www.msp-officialsite.com for more information on MSP.

Portfolio, Programme and Project Offices (P3O) (TSO, 2008) is aimed at helping organizations to establish and maintain appropriate business support structures with proven roles and responsibilities.

Visit www.p3o-officialsite.com for more information on P3O.

Structured project management methods, such as PRINCE2 (PRojects IN Controlled Environments) (TSO, 2009) or the Project Management Body of Knowledge (PMBOK) developed by the Project Management Institute (PMI), can be used when improving IT services.

Visit www.prince-officialsite.com for more information on PRINCE2.

Visit www.pmi.org for more information on PMI and PMBOK.

9.9 SKILLS FRAMEWORK FOR THE INFORMATION AGE

The Skills Framework for the Information Age (SFIA) supports skills audit, planning future skill requirements, development programmes, standardization of job titles and functions, and resource allocation.

Visit www.sfia.org.uk for further details.

9.10 CARNEGIE MELLON: CMMI AND ESCM FRAMEWORK

The Capability Maturity Model Integration (CMMI) is a process improvement approach developed by the Software Engineering Institute (SEI) of Carnegie Mellon University. CMMI can be used to guide process improvement across a project, a division or an entire organization.

The eSourcing Capability Model for Service Providers (eSCM-SP) is a framework developed by ITSqc at Carnegie Mellon to improve the relationship between IT service providers and their customers.

For more information, see www.sei.cmu.edu/cmmi/

9.11   BALANCED SCORECARD

The balanced scorecard approach provides guidance for what companies should measure to provide a balanced view. The balanced scorecard suggests that the organization be viewed from four perspectives, and it is valuable to develop metrics, collect data and analyse the organization relative to each of these perspectives:

- The learning and growth perspective
- The business process perspective
- The customer perspective
- The financial perspective.

Further details are available through the balanced scorecard user community at www.scorecardsupport.com

9.12   SIX SIGMA

Six Sigma is a data-driven process improvement approach that supports continual improvement. The objective is to implement a measurement-oriented strategy focused on process improvement and defects reduction. A Six Sigma defect is defined as anything outside customer specifications.

There are two primary sub-methodologies within Six Sigma: DMAIC (Define, Measure, Analyse, Improve, Control) and DMADV (Define, Measure, Analyse, Design, Verify). DMAIC is an improvement method for existing processes for which performance does not meet expectations, or for which incremental improvements are desired. DMADV focuses on the creation of new processes.